MINNIE BRUCE PRATT

Walking Back Up Depot Street
P　　O　　E　　M　　S

University of Pittsburgh Press

The publication of this book is supported by a grant
from the Pennsylvania Council on the Arts.

Published by the University of Pittsburgh Press, Pittsburgh, Pa.15261
Copyright © 1999, Minnie Bruce Pratt
All rights reserved
Manufactured in the United States of America
Printed on acid-free paper
10 9 8 7 6 5 4 3 2 1

A CIP catalog record for this book is available from the Library of Congress
and the British Library.

In memory of Audre Lorde and Muriel Rukeyser

Walking Back Up Depot Street

PITT POETRY SERIES

Ed Ochester, Editor

Language
is not a vague province. There is a poetry
of the movements of cost, known or unknown •

—William Carlos Williams,
Paterson, Book Three: "The Library"

Contents

PROLOGUE

In Hollywood, California (she'd been told), women travel
on roller skates, pull a string of children, grinning, gaudy-
eyed as merry-go-round horses, brass-wheeled
under a blue canopy of sky.
                                        Beatrice had never
lived in such a place. This morning, for instance, beside
Roxboro Road, she'd seen a woman with no feet wheel
her chair into fragile clumps of new grass. Her legs ended
at the ankle, old brown cypress knees. She furrowed herself
by hand through the ground. Cars passed. The sky stared down.
At the center of the world's blue eye, the woman stared back.

Years revolved, began to circle Beatrice, a ring of burning eyes.
They flared and smoked like the sawmill fires she walked past

      as a child, in the afternoon at four o'clock, she and a dark woman,
      past the cotton gin, onto the bridge above the railroad tracks.
      There they waited for wheels to rush like the wings of an iron angel,
      for the white man at the engine to blow the whistle. Beatrice had waited
      to stand in the tremble of power.

                                        Thirty years later she saw
the scar, the woman who had walked beside her then, split
but determined to live, raising mustard greens to get through
the winter. Whether she had, this spring, Beatrice did not know.
If she was sitting, knotted feet to the stove, if the coal had lasted,
if she cared for her company, pictures under table glass,
the eyes of children she had raised for others.

                                         If Beatrice went back
to visit at her house, sat unsteady in a chair in the smoky room,
they'd be divided by past belief, the town's parallel tracks,
people never to meet even in distance. They would be joined
by the memory of walking back up Depot Street.

                                         She could sit
and say: *I have changed, have tried to replace the iron heart*
with a heart of flesh.

                         But the woman whose hands had washed her,
had pulled a brush through her hair, whose hands had brought her maypops,
the green fruit and purple flowers, fierce eyes of living creatures—
What had she given her, that woman, anything all these years?

Words would not remake the past. She could not make it
vanish like an old photograph thrown onto live coals.

If she meant to live in the present, she would have to work, do
without, send money, call home long distance about the heat.

DOWN SOUTH

"We were landed up a river a good way from the sea ... where we saw few or
none of our native Africans ... I had no person to speak to that I could
understand. ... I was very much affrighted at some things I saw, and the more so
as I had seen a black woman slave ... cruelly loaded with various kinds of iron
machines; she had one particularly on her head, which locked her mouth so fast
that she could scarcely speak; and could not eat nor drink."
—*Olaudah Equiano*

Even before the flat yellow sail of the sun
passed beyond the horizon, Beatrice had stopped
looking. Fog had whited out details,
blurred the landscape, an overexposed photograph.

For that day she had seen enough. She had seen too much.
In the morning she'd worked in a room where arched light fell
unhindered on broken plaster. She'd stood at the blackboard
cuffed by what she was supposed to teach.

She had not drawn the blinds while they had talked
of the Middle Passage: the Yoruba, the Fulani, the Ibo,
the Bambara caught by men as white as ghosts
who shipped some on deck and most in the hold,

who decided which would have sunlight and which the dark
where children drowned in their own excrement, where
men and women remembered another kind of night
spent on their knees beside their mothers' graves,

the air thick with cries and the spirits of those
who had gone before, as wine glittered on the ground
to reconcile living and dead under the moon.
A thousand miles out they were led in coffles to the deck.

There some refused enslavement of their night and day.
They fled into the sea, dived into depths where light
came from no one direction but was present everywhere,
where blackness was refracted into countless shades.

Home for the evening, Beatrice wished to see no more.
She tried to walk out into an uncomplicated dark, down
to the deserted farmhouse to pick the last of the zinnias.
In the garden, pale blooms floated, like specks of foam.

Her hands had to grasp in the shadows for other flowers.
She thought she held burnt orange, red and fuchsia
set on tough green stems. She stood until
she began to see, plain as in the hour after dawn,

the petals, the color of each flower in the night.

A sign passed on her way to work:
Central Prison Renovation. A lie.
Old work, not new. No creation. A repetition
of walls, a dry well, people at the bottom,
a narrowed sky, few stars. Workmen in mid-air
laid down brick over brick, over hidden
doorways, barred exits. The new death
chamber would be ready by spring.

A white man leaned as usual from the tower,
his gun and his binocular eyes trained on
whatever escaped, any hand rapid
in the sun, delicate as a blue-black lizard
over sand.
                    At night the guards swiveled
eyes like klieg lights on a movie set,
watching for the shadow of a body to jump
at a corner of fence, over barbwire.

Right now the cement yard was as empty
as they could make it, except an edge of weed
at the wall. Inside the fence, the cells
were stacked, unfinished, like a paper wasp nest.

Days, as she drove to work, Beatrice
watched them be sealed, one by one,
with a silver wall. In a month they'd be filled
with men. Fifteen on death row, mostly Black.
Though the next death scheduled was a woman,
white, from out in the country by St. Paul's.

Velma put rat poison in her boyfriend's beer
their evening out, going to a gospel show.
Baffled neighbors said softly, again, *So nice!*

Evenings, lately, Beatrice stayed in.
                                        Days,
she watched some pokeweed sprout by the fence, coming
from dirt, from rain that rolled off the oily cement.
A plant you'd have to dig up by the roots to kill,
it grew spiraling: green stem, green leaf, white flower,
purple-black berry. When it got taller, the guards
would cut it back. No shade for the yard.
                                        Time
in the slow sun for those inside. No sudden moves.
Velma like bleached clothes hung out to dry.
The men, separate, hunkered against the wall.

On her way to work Beatrice saw the pokeweed grow.
She wished she was a mockingbird in the pokebush
so she could eat a berry and fly away, gone home.

on Sunday, anniversary of her death.

Beatrice folded the paper back to read more. The pages
flapped in her hands, loquacious tongues in the wind.

In the noon sun, the steady glare, she wondered if
the statue had bouffant hair, if the eyes were blank, if people
would walk by and point and laugh and stare at:

*Life-size bronze bust, local heroine, former attorney
general's wife, gained notoriety during Nixon years.*

Just her head and breasts, not even the whole woman.
Not like the metal heroes in this park, who had legs
with horses between them, who were armed, swords, flags
in their hands. They had the ground under them, and families
in front of them, bending to read the bronze plaques.

The dead presidents, governors, generals, the men
with mouths soldered shut, did not have to say
a word. The world grew orderly around them: grass
greened into rectangles, and stopped at brick walks.

Martha Mitchell didn't know when to stop
talking. That was her problem. Beatrice could hear
the men in Pine Bluff talking back: *Where's her
telephone? Wan'ut her mouth bigger than that?*

She clenched her teeth. Old words, grit in her mouth.

She'd said too much. That doctor, the dinner party.
She'd argued some men sometimes hit their wives, and
how did he know? Even his father, maybe, suddenly.

Suddenly. Words protruded from her mouth like teeth.
The other guests stepped away. She was an animal
in from the bushes, scavenger possum, bitter hisses
on their porch. They'd stiffened like wire screen against
her mean snout. Her face was all mouth.

And she had wanted to bite. She was tired of polite
letters to the editor, two hundred fifty words, no more,
in columns like ornamental borders, like the women
who lined government square Saturday afternoons.
They rallied at empty buildings, they railed at men not there
about their rights. She was tired of petitions like prayers.

Her mother had said: *If you don't believe in God, you'll*
go crazy. Told her: *You've got to hold onto something,*
a foundation.

After supper her mother held the floor
down with her feet as she knitted. Needles like knives
in her hands, clicking, cutting, eating up fear.

If she held her mouth the wrong way, the room would twist
inside out. The wind would strip her bare. There'd be
no floor, no wall, no door to open to another
life. That's what happened if you said you didn't believe.

Her mother knitted.

Her right-hand neighbor prayed:
Please fix it. Then the president spoke, a radio
voice in her ear. Told her to call the governor
about the light bill. Told her to yell at the power
company man: *I'll snatch your eyeballs out.*
She said a little spirit followed her and
as she walked it went *tat-tat-tat* in her ear.

Her own mouth working.

Maybe Martha Mitchell
talked to herself about what she knew. The president
a liar, her husband a thief. Muttered bourbon-and-coke
on the patio, shaking the ice cubes like dice. Maybe
a jaybird flew onto the grass, its eye a hard bead
with the gleam of knowledge. Then two blue wings flew it
out of the yard. Maybe that's how she decided law
was a room those men made, to walk in and out
like god, when they pleased.

She practiced at night, threw
words like ropes out her bedroom window. If she heard
a syllable hit the ground, she called reporters at day-
break. Her facts crawled on all fours to the front page.

Everyone said she was crazy. Beatrice had thought so.
The way her eyes darted and flicked like snakes' tongues
on TV talk shows.

The men sat in a room. On the screen
her mouth opened, a howl of scorn, and they scattered
like pieces of paper. But then she watched herself

disappear, shocked, drugged, shut off, a TV
re-run in a fading room.

The bust bears
a Bible verse: You shall know the Truth and the Truth
shall make you free.

In this country, you can have truth
by the mouthful, unspoken. Grind the words until they break.
Swallow them, cut your throat. Then say: *May I?*

But when
Beatrice changed sides, it was more like red rover, backyard games,
summer nights, her hand sweating in a girl's hand, her name called.

It was sitting on a couch with her lover, the room cool
as a cave, watching the other women kiss. Wind shook

the slatted blinds. It was night inside and out,
her feet at a bottomless edge. Soon sheets and the bed
would not hold her, falling naked. Her body funneled
toward truth. She wanted to. She was afraid.

Crazy,
the men said, slamming the door between her and her children.
She heard the wind rush past her head.

Sometimes
they lock you in. Sometimes they lock you out.

But she knew women who'd gone and done it anyway.

The white school teacher after the iron sound blew up
the church, scattered the mouths, the small teeth, the brown
ears, the breasts of four girls so young their nipples were eyes
not yet open to the world. Whose whisper in her ear was:
Go down and testify.

Who at the courthouse held up her sign:
Remember the children. Thirty-two years I have lived a lie.

Whose legs were steady as a statue dressed decent in brown suit,
brown gloves, brown paper bag over its head. Who took the bag
off in jail to talk. Who said she was a sign to others. Whose husband
bailed her out, sent her away to the madhouse, as he'd sworn.

Beatrice folded the paper to walk back to work where
the man at the next desk would say, *When I try to talk sweet,*
you go off like a gun in my face, rat-a-tat-tat.

Last night she dreamed she knelt on a sidewalk
and held a man's head in her hands. She thought
he was the governor. She thought he was the
president. She beat his head up and down until
the concrete cracked his skull. Blood flooded out,
nimbus for his white face, anger's halo, the circle
ground into the threshing floor at last judgment
when a mule is the god that tramples out the chaff.

Swingblade

She swung the red-rust triangle blade
up, back down, through the long grass.
The saw-teeth bit with a slow *shush, shush*.
She was getting used to the edge in her hand.

The next-door lady thought snakes might run
in the weeds. Beatrice had other fears.
The blade's weight pulled her arms down,
pendulum. The rhythm of slash in her hand.

If she had a dirt yard like some women back home,
she could sweep it morning and night with a switch,
scratch zig-zag circles until it was clean,
then make herself safe, slant lines in the sand.

For a month pumpkins had gathered at the curb market.
They sat on the ground, bigger than heads, orange
skins flawed, innocent. Going down to the store
to get some milk, Beatrice had watched them multiply.
Today she counted fewer. They were being bought
and carried away, but she did not want to own one.

She squatted down on the sidewalk. Under her palm,
rind was old leathery skin, hot as a stomach in the sun.
Her fingers remembered the small cave inside, the dark
slimy with seed, how the sides curved, muscular flesh
stored with summer water, memory of root and leaf.

Her right hand remembered the weight of a kitchen knife,
how the sides of the fruit had crunched under the blade.
She'd carved a sunken face, the glaring eyes, the angry grin.
She'd thought it was for the children, a harmless custom,
to set a fiery mask one night a year to guard her front steps,
a warning to wanderers: *You and you, keep out of my house.*

Her own face stared in the reverberating flame, her terror
that the knock at the door might be something come back
from the beyond, herself escaped from where she'd been locked.

On the threshold there might be a red-eyed, bear-faced woman
with moans whistling like wind through her yellow teeth,
the sounds she had made in pleasure before he called her *animal.*

Or a woman with no head, trying to tell, but no mouth to tell with,
how she felt underneath him, like a dead body under the coffin lid,
no thought, no want, her soul like someone else's eyes watching.

Or, at the door, a naked woman, body bent like a fig tree,
a pulp of afterbirth bloody between her legs, a child hanging
from each hand, their skins already soft as fruit with decay.

She couldn't keep the ghost of herself from reappearing,
the one who'd wanted sex anyway, though she'd been burned,
drowned, stoned to death for it in some other life. Not a story
she'd heard as a girl. Her mother never said out loud, *Don't
do it!* Just stood in their home like a stone angel staring
down on the graveyard.

                    Any Halloween she dressed up
she knew not to ask for a costume like the one hung
in the dime store window, purple sequin dress, feathered mask,
blood-red mouth and fingers.

                    Loose women had red nails.
             Their hands took what they wanted. What they got
             was fruit like ashes in the mouth. They were greedy
             and selfish. When they spread their legs, they got
             what they deserved, pregnant, backseat of a Chevy.
             They were cheap. They used men for their own
             reasons. Whatever they had was not theirs to give.

Past the store at the corner she lingered beneath the magnolia
to pick up a ripe cone with flushed folds, with scores of mouths,
a tongue of seed in each. The red fingers of seed pressed
into vulval curves.

                    Last night she lay down with a lover.
      Rooted in each other, their bodies branched up into vast night,
      dirt to sky, seen to unseen, taller than grandiflora.

Into the cave of that woman's body Beatrice reached her hand,
and it came away red, the nails outlined in blood, fingers
smelling of salt and iron hematite, a vein of ore, of ocean.

Tonight was the night the veil hung thin between the worlds.
Tonight a different woman might come back.

She kneels and stretches
over her, unfolds vulva, unveils sex smeared with blood.
Her two hands grip Beatrice, pull up her head to mark
forehead, eyes, mouth red

as seed pulp crushed
under this old tree. Once she walked down a red clay road
past a tree like this. The familiar was strange in the dark.

The fallen seeds were sweet turpentine, all that was left of white
blossoms that browned after a touch. Underfoot, dry leaves
crackled like small bones. The night grew colder and she ran
past the tree to get to her aunt's house. The windows were carved
squares of light in the darkness, just down the hill, around the curve,

no farther from where she was then, than she is now to

the two white men in an old car, driving by. One man sticks
a plastic skeleton out the window, clacks its mouth, and laughs.

Button

Saying hello, bottom step of the front steps,
her lover slid something small into her hand,
like who's-got-the-button, a shared secret,
the way she sometimes gave Beatrice a thought.

The something was cold as rain hitting their cheeks.
It was hard as bone, as the fingers of their held hands.
It was round as acorns before they bounced in the streets,
got crushed to smears of yellow meal, wasted.
It was round as an acorn rooting in the ground.

Beatrice faced her lover and unfolded her hand.
The acorn was brown, cracked at one end
like a hatching egg by a root or a sprout,
a tongue tasting rain in the livening dirt.

"The more I studied the situation, the more I was convinced that the
Southerner had never gotten over his resentment that the Negro was no
longer his plaything, his servant, and his source of income. The federal laws
for Negro protection passed during Reconstruction times had been made a
mockery by the white South where it had not secured their repeal.... It
seemed horrible to me that death in its most terrible form should be meted
out to the Negro.... For all these reasons it seemed a stern duty to give the
facts I had collected to the world."
—*Ida B. Wells-Barnett*

At first she thought the lump in the road
was clay thrown up by a trucker's wheel.
Then Beatrice saw the mess of feathers.

Six or seven geese stood in the right-of-way, staring
at the blood, their black heads rigid above white throats.
Unmoved by passing wind or familiar violence, they fixed
their gaze on dead flesh and something more, a bird on the wing.

It whirled in a thicket of fog that grew up from fields plowed
and turned to winter. It joined other spirits exhaled before dawn,
creatures that once had crept or flapped or crawled over the land.

Beatrice had heard her mother tell of men who passed
as spirits. They hid in limestone caves by the river, hooded
themselves inside the curved wall, the glistening rock.
Then just at dark they appeared, as if they had the power
to split the earth open to release them. White-robed, faceless
horned heads, they advanced with torches over the water,
saying, *We are the ghosts of Shiloh and Bull Run fight!*

Neighbors who watched at the bridge knew each man by his voice
or limp or mended boots but said nothing, let the marchers
pass on. Then they ran their skinny hounds to hunt other
lives down ravines, to save their skins another night
from the carrion beetles, spotted with red darker than blood,
who wait by the grave for the body's return to the earth.

Some years the men killed scores, treed them in the sweetgums,
watched a beast face flicker in the starry green leaves.
Then they burned the tree.

                              Smoke from their fires
still lay over the land where Beatrice traveled.

Out of this cloud the dead of the field spoke to her,
voices from a place where women's voices never stop:

>   *They took my boy down by Sucarnochee Creek.*
>   *He said, "Gentlemen, what have I done?"*
>   *They says, "Never mind what you have done.*
>   *We just want your damned heart." After they*
>   *killed him, I built up a little fire and laid out*
>   *by him all night until the neighbors came*
>   *in the morning. I was standing there when*
>   *they killed him, down by Sucarnochee Creek.*

>   *I am a mighty brave woman, but I was getting*
>   *scared the way they were treating me, throwing rocks*
>   *on my house, coming in disguise. They come to my bed*
>   *where I was laying, and whipped me. They dragged me*
>   *out into the field so that the blood strung across*
>   *the house, and the fence, and the cotton patch,*
>   *in the road, and they ravished me. Then they went*
>   *back into my house and ate the food on the stove.*

They have drove me from my home. It is over
by DeSotoville, on the other side in Choctaw.

I had informed of persons whom I saw
dressing in Ku Klux disguise;
had named the parties. At the time
I was divorced from Dr. Randall
and had a school near Fredonia.
About one month before the election
some young men about the county
came in the nighttime; they said
I was not a decent woman; also
I was teaching radical politics.
They whipped me with hickory withes.
The gashes cut through my thin dress,
through the abdominal wall.
I was thrown into a ravine
in a helpless condition. The school
closed after my death.

From the fog above the bloody entrails of the bird, the dead flew
toward Beatrice like the night crow whose one wing rests on the evening
while the other dusts off the morning star. They gave her such a look:

Child, what have you been up to while we
were trying to keep body and soul together?

But never mind that now. Here's what you must do:

Tie a red flannel string around your waist.
Plant your roots when the moon is dark. Remember
your past, and ours. Always remember who you are.
Don't let those men fool you about the ways of life
even if blood must sign your name.

The Blue Cup

Through binoculars the spiral nebula was
a smudged white thumbprint on the night sky.
Stories said it was a mark left by the hand
of Night, that old she, easily weaving
the universe out of milky strings of chaos.

Beatrice found creation more difficult.
Tonight what she had was greasy water
whirling in the bottom of her sink, revolution,
and one clean cup.

                She set the blue cup
down on the table, spooned instant coffee, poured
boiling water, a thread of sweetened milk. Before
she went back to work, she drank the galaxy that spun
small and cautious between her chapped cupped hands.

A Cold Not the Opposite of Life

"It is not accidental then, that where the Negroes are most oppressed, the position of the whites is also most degraded.... 'White supremacy' [in the South] means the nation's greatest proportion of tenants and sharecroppers, its highest rate of child labor, its most degrading and widespread exploitation of women, its poorest health and housing record, its highest illiteracy ... its highest death and disease rates.... Sharecropping has drawn into its orbit tens of thousands of poor white farmers."

—*Harry Haywood*

Nothing but pine boards between her and wind that would not stop blowing. She heard it come again from beyond the ridge, heavy and cold, moving tree limbs with the voice of dead leaves.

She had spent the day alone in this house, someone else's house. The pipes had frozen, the dishwater in the sink. The begonias died as if left out on the porch. From their puddled leaves came the smell of new mown grass. Snow lay, a thick white skin, on the pasture, on the road. She was stranded. Always before she'd been able to visit and leave.

Today she went out to the shed for wood, following a path made by another, a story:

> *The first snow I saw*
> *Mama would not let me do anything at all.*
> *Not put my hand out in the mystery, nor use*
> *a spoon to taste the whiteness, nor walk in it*
> *since one of my shoes had a hole. I waited at the window*
> *and it melted in the sun. It turned invisible, as I waited.*

The stove stoked, Beatrice stood at the window where other women had looked out before her. Silence fell in drifts on the brown grass, on the last clumps of green at this end of the county.

                                                    She had a summer picture
of a woman who'd lived in this place:

                              On the porch, screen door
            ajar behind her, three children barefoot, staring,
            her feet heavy in white pumps, black hair braided
            and crowned, print dress strained over her next child,
            short sleeves tight over muscled upper arms,
            hands enormous and full of the baby on her lap.

Beatrice had facts about her from a book:

                              Home
            of a tenant farmer, mother of the family, thirty-three
            years old, married at twenty-one, four children
            from six months to nine years, a sharecropper all her life.

Through neighbors still living, Beatrice heard her last words:

            She'd split out of her clothes like a grasshopper
            with every child, but hadn't yelled with any.
            She'd grunted it out because if you yell on a pain,
            you'll have it over. Anyway, if you yell too much,
            you'll kill the baby. Before she married, her papa
            had said she was his best hand. She could plow, cut
            and maul wood, harrow, do everything a man could.

            But if you've got to be taking care of children too,
            housework is easier, although there's always cooking,
            cleaning, washing, milking, churning, sewing, canning,
            and the children. Really, if it weren't for worrying
            over them, she'd rather've been working outdoors anytime.
            She was brought up to it. Most years they planted forty-

thousand hills of tobacco, five thousand an acre,
with sweet potatoes, field peas, corn, and cane for syrup.

One year Papa's death kept them from getting
the fodder off the cane. The leaves had carried the frost
right down to the heart of the stalk and killed it.
One year the beetles ruined all the beans. That made it
harder to scrape up a meal three times a day.
She never had no noon, and many a night stayed up,
without company, to tend the fire in the curing barn.

When she was younger, she'd had her a girlfriend.
Still wore her gold brooch with the picture taken
together when they were eighteen. They used to go
into town to sell blackberries, and eggs and butter,
with a bunch of girls, as they were afraid of the negroes.
After she married, her husband did all the buying
and selling. She managed inside the house,
he managed the outside. That was no place for a woman.

After the last baby, she hadn't visited much
except to go to funerals. It wasn't her fault
she had so many children. She'd never enjoyed it.
When nature left her, she still knew what
was going on down there, but at least
she didn't feel a thing. He'd always treated
her just like she was a beast, didn't care
how many babies he made her have.
She had ten surviving, and one dead, had passed it
in the evening, walking home from the field.
She'd had on overalls so no one noticed, but
she hadn't felt the same inside since.

She'd raised the others, pulled them right up
by the hair of their head. When they were little

she used to go outside and watch the stars.
Then she'd thought: They'd been there before her
and would be when she was gone. So she stopped
going out. She'd tried to be content with her lot.
She'd done the best she could and you can't do
more than that. But sometimes she'd got tired.

Beatrice had heard this voice in the mouths of many women.
She carried it around inside her. She put another slab of pine on
and tried instead to listen to the fire, its yellow, red,
black flame, its insect buzz.

The windows thickened with ice,
the pasture blurred. She did not want to get a ten-foot stare
in a twelve-foot room, to lose focus at the wall and fall silent.

In this house with no closets all possessions were exposed: the hatchet
on the mantle with a hornets' nest, the jars of preserves stacked
on the floor. She did not want these oddities of light to be
more substantial than the shadow of her heart. Nor did she want
her body stretched out like a white field under someone else's hand.

When she stepped outside, she did not want the horizon to vanish
into a waste of white until she feared anything at the field's edge.
She wanted to see what she looked at. The old directions to the farm
were *down the road, third house on the right.* On the way she'd seen
five. Where dark people lived had not been counted.

She would cast her own shadow on the white killing frost,
to come to a cold not the opposite of life, like a walk
to the creek, beyond the pasture.

There, above the beaver dam,
water lay in waves of ice. Its flow caught past seasons,
fragments of dead leaves. It sealed green algae still breathing,
the beaver with her store of sweet-barked twigs. It was the cold
necessary to break the sleep of seeds.

She would live
in change,
the cold to break at the bottom of the marsh, the wind
to remind her: *There is something different from you dwelling here.*

Out of Season

In the backyard, earthworms had migrated,
tunneled down the morning that ice grew up
like spikes of red grass through the dirt.
Below the frostline they raveled together,
a ball of twine waiting for the sun
to pull them to the surface in the spring.

But Beatrice did not want to wait. Light
slithered from the beveled edge of her mirror
into bands of red, indigo, violet
as she set out to anticipate nature.
She potted up four narcissus bulbs
and put them in the brief winter of a closet.

Roots circled in the dark, pressed pale
reptilian stomachs against the clay.
Brought to the window, leaves began to rise
striped green and white, garter snakes
in a glass jar when she was five.
Then paper hoods split around white mouths,

and on the table flowers loomed, cobras
summoned from a basket by the secret word.
For days Beatrice enjoyed their scent
and her power to charm them into form
out of season, inside her time.
By the tick of her banjo clock she lured

narcissus into her room in mid-winter.

She stepped into the building, a blue trapezoid,
as shiny as a skink's tail, more grey than the sky-blue
eggs laid by the paper wasp in the cells of its nest,
more like the milky indigo of certain mushrooms.

Some folk would think this blue a fine color
for a man-made building, or the sky, but unnatural
for mushrooms, would say filth out of rotting dirt
should be brown. Beatrice thought of the way
people confused nature with their own ideas,
lived in contraries, but wanted to see things simple.

Any day she could walk out her back door and see
things weren't simple. This morning in the vacant lot
the ground was covered by circles, a fallen
tree stump dividing into particles, fungus
breeding elemental dirt, cold and alive.

The dirt would change itself after a warm spell,
a slow rain, into clumps of smooth brown eggs
ready to hatch, invisible spores to sprout and
decay, to make more dirt where green leaves
poked out like grasshopper wings, sweetgum
trees to stand again taller than twenty people,
green, red, purple-black against a blue sky.

Standing on that ground, Beatrice couldn't tell beginning from end,
what was dirt, what was blue, what was her.
Inside the tinted glass she felt
out of place, dirty jeans, dirt in her fingernails. She could see no leaves
ever blew in on this floor.

She passed by chairs plastic as ideas
in the lobby. She passed by cubicles where old men taught young men
the forms, white numbers chalked on blackboards, how to abstract, how
their minds set them apart from gross matter. They discussed the sun,
the moon's surface, like real estate agents, as they sat in narrow desks,

the kind she'd hardly fit in when she was at school, pregnant one year,
always the wrong shape. She got from class to class holding up her head,
pretending she was not her swollen stomach that grew and pulled
and pulled, like it would pull her down. She'd tried to be not herself.

Like Manya Sklodovska in her textbook, the Slav, the foreign
woman, who boiled pots of pitch, stirred eight tons of ore to isolate
a hidden purity, a white powder, some part of matter with the power
to transmute itself into another world, immense, perhaps immortal.

The Manya who made herself Marie, a Frenchwoman, scientific,
rational, whose radium glimmered like glowworms in a rotten log.
Marie who had the marrow in her bones burned away by light
pulled up out of its dirt.

Was it suicide, she wondered,
if you killed yourself by changing from dirty body to pure mind?
At twelve she knew breasts were the opposite of thinking. Could have
murdered hers.
In school she got close to mind only
because she was white. Everyone knew that thought was white.
Like light. Contrary to body. Bodies were death.
Yet here
she was, and here were her breasts, wary, but prancing slightly
as she walked.

Down the hall people circled, chanting: *The human race!* They were waiting for a man who'd killed tens of thousands with his mind.

Beyond them Beatrice saw photographs flash on the wall, a chain of actions from the year she was born:

*A bomb fell through air. The pilot veered
up from incandescent light, a puffball
of dust. The button of a mushroom emerged
at ground level, swelled with its own heat,
stalked and spread its cap, released spores
of invisible poison. Buildings imploded.*

*People fell dead as light sucked air
from their lungs with a roar. Others burned.
Clothes melted into their skin, they lay
charred wood beside the road. Some endured
the instant of time printed on their flesh. A man
with face shadowed by cherry leaves. A woman
with breast scarred by butterflies from her kimono,
negatives left on the sensitive film of skin.*

*Later children kicked on sheets with too many
arms and legs, born like beetles or grasshoppers
with tiny heads, shriveled hearts. Then
a grown woman with folded pubis, no bigger than
the bud of a five-year-old girl, between her thighs.*

Horror between her thighs, in her stomach, coming up, breath scorching, withering her lungs. She shouldn't scream, not in public. She wasn't a child. And it was an orderly demonstration.

A little white man nodded through the crowd, father of the bomb,
head huge as the globe. He wore his skin like a summer suit.

No need to go hear him. He'd sound like her father, telling
stories to scare her.

> *Beyond the porch in the night*
> *were black wizened men. Their eyes were fiery coals.*
> *Their hands were metal claws.*

> He'd say: *Be careful.*
> *They'll get you and turn you into them.*

Or he'd flash
slides like the movie matinee on Saturday afternoon. The bomb
explodes in a desert, lower life goes wild, giant grasshoppers
gnaw down power lines, electrocute themselves, but white hero,
heroine press unmutated mouths together and live.

Then
he'd close with a moral, voice of apocalypse on Sunday morning.
How those who know as beasts, naturally, who follow strange
flesh, the filthy dreamers who despise dominion, would burn,
ashes of Sodom and Gomorrah, wells without water, trees
of withered fruit, twice dead.

No need to go to listen
to this famous man. No matter what he said, his voice
would promise salvation by skin.

He would never tell her about
afterwards:

That while she was walking barefoot up a sandy creek,
to follow its thread of light into green shadows, the sweetbay thicket,
invisible ashes were falling on her skin, her unbudded breasts,
radium blown south by prevailing winds.

He would never
tell her she was us and them, that opposites did not have
to kill each other off.

On summer afternoons her father
killed wasps with a folded newspaper. *Get them before they
get you,* he slammed.

In the hall, the door shut behind the scientist.
People dropped silent to the floor, crumpled like a heap of defeated
bodies.

Beatrice looked at despair and walked out. She wouldn't
lie down and die. She would act contrary somehow, like the wasps
that fought the front porch screen, battered by light on the other side
brighter than anything. They'd sting you like a knife, if they had to, to live.

The White Star

Inside the White Star it was warm, tumbled clothes
and humming revolution of unsteady washer-dryers.
It was a whirligig blur of red black blue yellow
that Beatrice watched like a TV, next to her lover.

Last night she'd looked into lighted windows
bitterly, as if she'd been evicted, things thrown
out on the sidewalk, cracked lamp, books sprawled
by the mattress, sheaves of paper spilled, all
looking small and naked, exposed, like her once
in a bad dream of childhood.

                      Not yet, except
they'd been kicking some people out on her street,
not her, not yet, not for skin or rent money,
but always perhaps if she forgot to draw her curtains
when she kissed the woman who was not her sister,
when they slowdanced in the kitchen before supper.

Not yet, but already to her. The children taken,
no place of hers, lit or dark, fit for home.

Not yet here to her, but already to a white woman
on the block, standing out by her clothes piled out
to draggle-tail in the dirt, in the getting-dark time,
clouds neon pink, birds going to roost so fast
they leave only a single wingbeat in the air overhead.

Already to a brown woman under a mound of blankets
piled by the corner, her head emerging at footsteps,
cautious, fearful, wrinkled turtle neck.

                                      Already
to the sallow woman on a laundry bench, wine skin
hot as a blanket, asleep in the clean drunk room.

Tonight in the White Star muzak was playing old
brittle raindrops. Beatrice leaned sideways against
her lover, smelling her hair and the clean clothes.
Next bench, a man muttered stones, a woman stared away.

        The padlocked doors, people bending in the rain
        to salvage one obscure object, people shouting
        to no one: *We live here. You can't throw us out.*

    She closed her eyes and wished they could dance
    in this lit public place. Mouth against the other's ear,
    she began to hum: *Go in and out the window, go in*
    and out. How the glass would crack under a desperate fist.
    Go in and out the window as we have done before—

The A & P

She rolled a tomato in her hand, pink rubber
ball engineered to fit a machine. The motion
recalled Florida, toward the Glades, Pahokee,
Belle Glade, Miccosukee, fields crawling
with tomato plants, and the proportion all wrong
between the rows: wide enough for a truck to drive
through. A truckload of migrant workers, Cuban,
Haitian, Jamaican, perhaps Creek, Seminole,
turning, rolling to a spot on the horizon, stopping
somewhere, the next unpicked spot the same,
on the row, assembly line.

A voice from somewhere
urban, in her ear: *We have forgotten where
our food comes from.*

But she remembered exactly.
Between the rows of manufactured produce she remembered
Lib Martin's bucket of tomatoes: green, red,
irregular skin cracked like red dirt, drought,
rain. The acid juice gushed against thirst.

Not forgetting. Learning certain things, like these sweet
potatoes, knobbed roots broken to yellow clay,
eating them baked as some ate clay, hot
from the sun, comfort. Sweet potatoes twenty cents a pound.

A man in Nash County died digging them last fall,
forty cents a bucket, seventy buckets a day, take out
a hundred fifty bucks a month for beans and rice.

Pull wild salad, fish the Tar River, drink
cheap wine, a dollar a pint. Can't escape,
beaten with tree limbs, the woods full of snakes. Be
so hot. Fall into dirt from your own digging, and die.

Not about forgetting. Never being told.

Eating the lives of others like a child, unconscious,
sucking the breast. Herself as a girl sucking
sugar cane by the gas heater, hot, sweet,
knowing nothing of the cold field, the knives of cane,
the women and the men, rounding the mill like mules.

But it was about forgetting. Every day she wanted to
forget something she'd learned about the house, the fields,
the lopped cedar posts propping up the scuppernong arbor,
the fallen grapes fermenting on the ground. If she could have,
just tonight, a little white wine. The amnesiac sugar,
liquor, how good it tastes. It used to be whiskey,
or a little rum-and-coke.

How drunk she got
that night, her and the two men, drunk, standing up
in the boat between two rivers of stars, between
the muddy banks of the Black Warrior.
They sang
until the boat sank, then waded out as if
free in another country. She'd washed the black muck
off her feet, clinging weight, erosion, lives
she knew, lives she did not know. She had walked
up the bank, stagger, not like her father. Just like
her father. What did he know?

Too much, her mother said,
he knows too much to be happy.

Drinking to forget
what he did, or what he should have done? At the river,
the river bottom land.

Maybe the grapefruit in her hand,
yellow globe, pink flesh, came from there, prison farm
in the bottoms. Hot boxes. Boxes of fruit. Each piece
wrapped like a jewel in green tissue paper.

She had learned about grapefruit, lemons, oranges.
In the store, workers unpack them like presents. Pesticide
spreads skin to skin, and your hands begin to die,
go numb, skin falls off, membrane of a peeled orange.

Stay conscious, a voice said. *Can't do nothing if you don't
stay conscious. Right foot should know what the left foot is doing.*

But every time, every damn time, she walked
into this A & P to get groceries, she had to decide
not to be like her father. Decide like tonight.
No grapefruit, no tomatoes, none of that Iowa honey,
bees that never saw a flower, their universe a warehouse.
Ask where the sweet potatoes came from. Then a few
in a paper sack, thudding like lumps of dirt.

Then her feet up and down aisles twice as wide
as a row should be hoed, making her feet take her
past, her hand not reach down a bottle, not even
the scuppernong that could give her back herself

innocent, under the arbor, sucking grapes down
to the skin, the familiar taste, numbness, a long
slow spiral down the river, oblivion's boat,
her feet never stepping out on either side of land.

She made herself walk past the wine, to check-out,
to figure up how much this food would cost her.
She could dig up the backyard again this spring,
some rows of tomatoes, some cane poles spiraling
bean vines. Some squash, three seeds and a fish head
at the bottom of each hole.
               The dead silver eye
would look at her again. Again she would ask herself
the use of what she was doing, and again as she hoed,
barefoot in blackjack clay, and as the tomatoes came in
to be picked, eaten, given to friends, canned for winter.
Again as the blisters came, and then the calluses on her hands.

The Possum Eats
Out of the Graveyard

"Friends, I want to tell you that the Scottsboro boys were framed by the bosses of the south and two girls. I was one of the girls and I want you to know that I am sorry I said what I did at the first trial, but I was forced to say it. Those boys did not attack me and I want to tell you all right here now that I am sorry that I caused them all this trouble for two years, and now I am willing to join hands with black and white to get them free."
—*Ruby Bates*

Night after night she has had bad dreams. She clicks the light
out. She sits on the bed afraid to sleep. She'll wake
up as the man opens a door to her room. Grey light.
His dark silhouette, her fate. She is always too late to turn
the lock. She crouches down like ducklings she once saw
at the zoo, huddled in fear of a child's kite. Just a shadow,
but hawk-winged to them on their pond, sudden death in its beak.

She tries to close the door on his claw. Then she wakes.
In daylight she knows better. She knows what she was taught.

One night she hears a hand scratch at the screen door, but
when she looks out back, it's only a possum from the green waste
beside the drainage ditch. It's looking for food.

                                                    At home
they say the possum is an evil thing. It eats the dead. It eats
out of the graveyard. Maybe it smells the bad blood in her dreams.

She sits on the edge of the bed in her hooked-up-the-front
bone-backed corset, face powdered for the first time, pollen-
cheeked, lips rouged pink as if already kissed. Waiting
to slide the horsehair net petticoat over her head. Pain,
excitement, someone's fingernails scratching along her thighs.

To put her arms up for the blue-green foam of evening gown,
hands in an arc as if to dive from the height above the creek,
the place where the boys risked death. But not yet. Hands
clasped tense in her lap, steadying for the plunge, her head
to emerge glistening from the strapless dress her mother held.

Waiting in the moment before, when nothing is smudged.
Her eyes wide, terror of mascara. Her father comes in from the kitchen.
He stands in front of her, hand at her neck. He slides one finger under
the corset breastplate, down her untouched skin, a finger of cold water.

He never touched her again. But he used to show her pictures.
If they were alone. Flashing photographs of a Black man
in a nice suit, walking with people down a street. Everyone
is holding hands. He'd say: *That man touches women.*
He puts his filthy hands on girls as young as you.

Grown, she sits on her bed, terrified. Someone is
coming. She cries out to her woman lover: *Do something.*
No answer. Unheard. A man comes in the room, a Black man,
mouth open. Anger? Danger? She runs. The house closes
into smaller and smaller rooms, add-ons, lean-tos. At a phone
she screams her lover's name, who answers, from the far end of hope:
I will come. Running, she is back at the beginning, the room with the man.
She comes in behind him. He waits in a chair. She sees just the slope
of his hair. Then, in a breath, his head splits open. A hand slowly
spreads blood on two slices of bread. A voice says: *Eat. That's what you want.*

The hand holds up a mirror to her face, but when she looks
she sees dead flesh, charred by fire. The voice says: *Look.*
This is what you'll see when you feel desire. This is what you'll fear.
Then the hand smashes the mirror and says: *Remember.*

She won't. She won't remember only that. Sitting up North
at tea, her friend had asked instead: *Did you ever hear
of Scottsboro?*

Before she was born, the year her mother turned
twenty. The two women about that age, the young men, younger.
Opposite ends of a train bound from one mill town to another.

A white girl in overalls sits in the boxcar's open door.
She waits to jump as the train slows down, before the sheriff
sees her. By law, she's a tramp unless she's got a father
or brother handy. And it's true last night she filled herself
with a man. In the slow night rain they shifted and slid, slick
on cardboard boxes, back under the honeysuckle. His weight
pressed into her hollows. She forgot hunger for an hour.

Down by the wheels, she and the other girl can see two ways:
the white man, the steel mouth of his shotgun, the jail floor,
or nine Black men. Closer, they're really just boys, younger
than them. One hardly can walk, dragging his leg, dead weight.
Another gropes with his hands, head tilted, eyes half shut.

If she lies and says they did it, she'll get food and pity,
a look that knows she's been fucked but says, *Poor trashy
thing, God bless her.* She can lie and she'll go free.

At forty, she rocks on a porch, coughs, takes a taste
of snuff for her cotton mouth, the saliva spurt. The mill's
closed, she's out of work again, though she could still
spool and spin with the best. As for that old story, well, what
do you want? She'll change her mind again if you've got
ready money. Only salt and cornmeal in the house, for hoecakes.

Meanwhile, they get sent to death, or life. While they wait
there is convict labor, the field or the mine, bales of cotton
to pick for the mills, tons of coal to dig. Coal to burn
the water, steam for the wheels to turn and the sparks to fly
electric, to run like fire through the lines to the mills and the state
prison chair where the jury hoped they would sit till their blood boiled dry.

One by one, they get out before they die, after twenty years
of days like the morning a thousand people, white and Black, most
in overalls, half-raggedy, walked toward the assembly hall, past
police with their box of tear gas bombs, under three machine guns
at the corner. The people walked on in the door to their meeting.
Nonchalant in numbers. And one white woman in the witness stand
wouldn't lie, said she wanted to be the one to tell the truth.
Truth walking in the street, by the thousands. She heard it, ruthless.
This time she would not be alone when she stepped down.

In the year when he'd been in jail for as long as he'd lived free
the oldest makes a break. Ten days on foot through creeks
he doesn't know the name of, he walks northeast to the city.
They hunt him with dogs. He hears their brassbell baying.
They hunt him with a silver airplane as he creeps in muck
he thinks will be his grave. Maybe someone with a truck
gives him a ride, maybe not. In the end someone else hides
him in a car trunk and smuggles him farther north, contraband.
He has four years left. Sees snow, cottondrift by the road. Writes a book.

A book spread open in her lap. White pages written over in blood.
The story of desires. He says his were simple, and not so different from hers.

She sits alone in the dark. Maybe in the night to come
she'll get up to let her lover in through the dream's back door.

On the Silver Coast

In the nightwood shadow she stood small as a big dog
at the fiery circle's edge, a rutted circle beaten in
the dirt, the mule going round and round hitched
to a lopped cedar pole gripped by iron bands, grinding
the cane down to juice clear as rainwater, to syrup
sweetened by a fire the men tended all night while
she waited for her taste.

                                           Deep in her shadowed bed
she licks that memory sticky from her lips. Nothing left but
memory, the bed barren as a stubble field. Lover has gone,
cold weather come on. Somewhere else a beach with sun.

She could reach there, hand on the other's breast, silk grit sand,
sip *coco frio*. She would get there just as someone's voice called
Madre! and night slid over the palms, the hibiscus, just as
the sulfur yellow sunset faded and one peacock screamed *Kee
yaw, kee yaw*, desperate in its loneliness, arrogant and angry.

She would breakfast on banana *niñas*, oranges *del pais*,
passion fruit sliced like boiled eggs, halves of orange yolk,
seeded soft morsels to grind and fill her ravenous mouth.
As the hummingbird bee, *zimbador*, enters the redslipper flower,
she would tongue, she would be mean claws. It would all
be hers.
                       In the bay's transparent water she would
raise the net and fling over silver *sardinas*, seine them
into the plastic bucket, their flapping death rattle, grim
satisfaction. Yes, she would have them, she would have her back.

The fishy smell, Bahía Media Luna. Rank tears down her face,
wet with salt. Nothing, no touch smeared between her legs, just
the years a paste in her mouth like plantain, *tostones*. Garlic
stinging, how her tongue would sear, numb as her hands
in the nettle she parted to get through to the water, to get

down to the forbidden beach, past the guard of soldiers, past
the gate where they run guns, where sugar boats once launched,
past the old fields where men walked round the track of mules,
to grind cane into silver for the ones who owned the sweetness.

The flash of El Dorado like a fish in water. Her craving:

It was in her, it was in me. How do I get it back?
Moving on top of her on top of me, pelvis
grinding over and over, please take it, please,
what is precious in me. Melt me and pour me.
Not myself. I will escape. I will be silver
ingot, hot liquid sound, Madre! *answered.*

I will be thrown net, palm frond rattling,
sound of rain quenched. Your salt hot tears
on my face, your bahía media luna. *I will get there*
though I see the island denuded of trees.

                            The bull-
dozer grinds over the sugarmill stones, while guns
fire at night, and fish, deafened, dead, float belly up,
silver undulations beyond the ruins.
                           By the kitchen
the cistern chokes, where crabs once crowded for the cook.
On the patio a fig tree still fruits by the broken machines,

scattered iron, bits not worth the five *centavo*
piece, mossy with verdigris, she finds on the hill.

The ruins mine, and mine alone. Nothing in my hand
and what I want I can not buy. Nothing will give me
your face turned to me, your tongue lapping. Hummingbird
nectar, delicious insects dying in a pool of sweetness
I can not get for myself. Take it and give it,
voracious tongue.

                       The breeze in and out of curtains,
languid, inexorable. *Ka ka   ka ka   ka ka   ka ka   ka ka*
koo koo, lizard cuckoo, take her there, the place she wants.

Rain bird, bring down sweetness and salt, day rain,
night rain, on the silver coast, all sweetness lost.

The cat sleeps with her, back to back,
a pool of molasses, spilled copper-
black, domestic at odd moments
in the night, sewing with curved needles
a secret buttonhole, humming.

With light, the cat watches the wall,
slit eyes spread a net. She hunts
plaster as if to rip it, skin
off lathing. Beatrice can not see
what the cat knows. Perhaps

the past taps like a deathwatch beetle
in the wood. Perhaps the rapid future
beats, invisible, the heart of a bird.

At Deep Midnight

"The legal legacy of slavery and of the seizure of land from Native American peoples is not merely a regime of property law that is (mis)informed by racist and ethnocentric themes. Rather the law has established and protected an actual property interest in whiteness itself."
—*Cheryl Harris*

It's at dinnertime the stories come, abruptly,
as they sit down to food predictable as ritual.
Pink lady peas, tomatoes red as fat hearts
sliced thin on a plate, cornbread hot, yellow
clay made edible. The aunts hand the dishes
and tell of people who've shadowed them, pesky
terrors, aging reflections that peer back
in the glass when they stand to wash up at the sink.

One sister shivers and fevers with malaria,
lowland by the river where Papa tries to farm
the old plantation. Midnight, she calls to him
to save her, there's money on fire, money between
her thighs, money burning her up, she's dying.

He brings no water but goes on his knees,
jerks up the bedclothes, shouts something she
has not said, has she? Yelling at the invisible man
he sees under the bed: *Come out from there, you
black rascal, you.* Flapping the heavy sheets
like angel wings, and smiling at his baby daughter

who in her eighties shuffles her words briskly
like a deck of playing cards, and laughs and says,
We're all crazy here, lived around negroes too long.

The oldest sister walks barefoot home from school
trembling. At the curve by the Lightsey's house
a Black woman stands, bloody-handed, holding up
a pale fetus from a slaughtered sow, laughing,
I've killed me a baby, lookit the baby I killed.

Beatrice looks past them all, sees the ramshackle houses
past her grandmother's yard, the porch tin cans of snakeplants.
Inside, sooty walls, from a hundred years of pineknot smoke.

Inside no bigger than a corncrib. The door shuts from outside.
They can hear the board drop into the slot, the angry man
shut in to stand stud, the woman on her back on cornshucks,
who later, bloody, smothers her new daughter in rough homespun.

Inside a white-washed, lamplit room, a man bends over
a ledger: *Boy Jacob Seventy-Five Dollars, Five Sows
and Sixteen Piggs Twenty Dollars.* His pen flickers:
how fast could the pair he bought cheap increase five-fold
because God had said replenish the earth and subdue it?

Now the aunts are asking about her children, the boy
babies who'd so pleased, with their white skin, silky
crisp as new-printed money, a good thing too, with the farm
lost long ago. Beatrice wonders if the youngest sister

remembers the noon she snapped the bedroom door open
on her, arched, aching, above the girl cousin, taking
turns on the carefully made-up bed. Flushed like dove
out of the room's dusty shade, they murmured denials.
They ended the long kissing that gets no children.

Her nipples had been brown-pink like a bitten-into fig,
gritty sweet, never tasted, lost as her cousin dressed
after a night they'd sunk together in the feather mattress
hip to hip, hair tangled, kinky brown, spring-coiled blonde,
skin stuck to humid skin in the sandy, damp sheets. Dressed,
at breakfast, elbow to elbow, they ate biscuits and jelly.

She never claimed her with a look, no wherewithal, no currency
in love, no madness, no money, only a silent vacancy.

Only the stupor of lying alone on the bed reading: *The man
takes the woman roughly in his arms, pushes her down.* If
she lay still enough, she might feel. Pressing herself
down. The bedspread's blunt crochet cuts into her face,
her cheek rouged and gouged by the thread's harsh twist.

They have more ice tea, the heat almost too much. The heat
at deep midnight grinds into slight motion, whir of a fan.

All sleeping, the aunts, the mother, the grown daughter. While
from bed to bed, slow as the sodden air, move two young girls,
white not-yet-swollen breasts, white underpants, white ghosts.

They stand at each bed, watching, asking, their dark, light
hair drifting like fire out from their unforgiving faces.

"[In 1955, during the Montgomery bus boycott mass arrests], Blacks had come from every section of town. Black women with bandannas on, wearing men's hats with their dresses rolled up. From the alleys they came, that is what frightened white people. Not the collar and tie group. I walked in there and the cops were trembling.... One of the police hollered, 'All right, you women get back.' These *great big old women* told him, and I never will forget their language, 'Us ain't going nowhere. You done arrested us preachers and we ain't moving.' He put his hands on his gun and his club. They said, 'We don't care what you got. If you hit one of us, you'll not leave here alive.'"
—B. J. Simms

In her birthplace, she's a tourist in the shrine to martyrs
for freedom, votive lights set before photographs,
newspaper names: Reeb, Liuzzo, Jimmie Lee Jackson.
Under the flicker of their stubborn eyes, she fingers
bare footprints, plaster casts on a museum table,
steps of unknown travelers set down by the riverside.
Those who climbed and crossed the bridge: maidservant,
carpenter, teacher, fieldhand, and no way to tell
who was who, no match between work and foot. Naked,
ready for cool water in a tin basin, someone to wash
off the dust. How beautiful upon the mountain the feet
of them that bring good. Arc of flesh heavy in her hand.

She has a dream sometimes she is walking the road
out of town, past the depot and the gin, on the road
to Selma, past burnt-up fields. The jaybird declares
to the crow, *Rain no more,* and the dry creek crawls.
Catfish gasp for breath, but the crawfish steadily
dredge the world up, scratching clay from underneath.

Going downhill she pours shade like water on her head,
slides her bare arm past briar jaws to pick dewberries.
Knife vines slit her skin, but each berry's a rough nipple
in her mouth, lost bliss. Kiss of memory sunk in her flesh,
imprint, sure as clay holds each foot ever on it, toes splayed
or heel of boot.

           She tastes the music a long ways off
as doors open, voices come down the road. She can almost
grasp the meaning, echo of people bound for the meeting.

We jumped rope with bramble briars, we'd peel
the thorns right off.
           In a little while gonna
turn back to dirt, don't matter how rich, we be
nothin but dirt.

       Worked for a lady once, she
was sweet, she was mud rich, so when everyone be gone,
and everything, she lost her mind over that land.
She said, We couldn't keep our place, our place.

Worked for a lady once, she played bridge, she sat
on her sofa to read poetry, didn't know we had
the same thing under our skirts.

          In our house, the hens
pecked through the floor cracks. I kept baby in a pasteboard
box under the gumtree. Water at noon.
Thank mercy, couldn't ever dip that spring dry.

I've tried to live a life I'm not ashamed of. A lie is
a lie, don't matter how you dress it up. I'm not
ashamed for my life to be on the air. Can you say that?

Beatrice follows behind, comes on three buzzards sitting
in the road. They grunt and hiss and flap. They rip some life
from a small dead animal, stinking, past.
                                        The field's
bone-dry, not enough water at the river to swim a dog.
Tracks at the water's edge, confusion, the mud-split hooves
of cows come to drink, and trample marks where people waded
out, no sure place where she can set her feet.

A voice calls back her way, *Soon we all gonna be
dirt, nothin but dirt, might as well join us.*

They say, *Are you ready to sleep in a cardboard box
on the cold clay ground, are you ready to stand ready
while we speak from a platform of coffins? Are you ready
to walk?*

                    The road turns. She turns aside, down a worn path
under barbwire. A Black man leaves as she sneaks through,
says, *No matter what, they'll say I raped you.* His foot and hand
stretch the fence jaws for her passage. *They'll tell you how often.
Forty-seven times. Remember I told you.*

                                        Property line.
White stile steps at another fence. Dirt road by the quarters,
paved road by the courthouse. In front the white men laugh,
No way out, you slut. Hands on their crotches, forking roads.

The road to Snow Hill where William Edwards walks to school
with bare bleeding feet, praying, *Summer, please come, wild plums.*

The road to Camp Hill where Ralph Gray stands with his shotgun
to guard the meeting place, vacant house in a cotton field.
Only the bloom of yellow eyes watch when the sheriff comes.

The road through Lowndes County, coming up on a car slewed
across. Through the mesh of broken glass the white woman's
blasted eyes search blindly for the dark riders she ferried,
can they reach safety?

Beatrice wants to be, wants to be
ready. The road through the courthouse, the room where her father
stands over her as she marks her ballot. White rooster. Black
panther. Somewhere in this long hall a hidden door. A woman hauling
a tin pail of water points, *Yes*.

Past her, the museum of shadows.
Light opens. A woman leaves, says, *I lived this, I can't watch it*.
The video whirs, pours out black-and-white people stumbling.

Through the window she sees rain come up a river that splits
and shakes like a leaf as the gulf wind hits it.

She sees children
beaten by fists of water. She sees people climb a mountain bridge
to stand in mist, tear gas, men on horseback with cattle prods.
The woman in the hallway whispers, *One way in, and one way out*.

Past the blank screen, she sees the other side of the water,
the riverbank and people gathered. Are they her people? Can't
see their faces. Once she ran here falling on soft grass, darkness.
The only light, fireflies and fire under iron cook kettles. Hot grease
smell, the promise of food for all, crisp fish. Glimmer of faces bent
over flame, marking her in place. Once. Once in the morning sunflash
she ran down to swim, and strangers stood knee-deep singing, *Come,*
in the muddy water, a song she knew, from unknown mouths. Now

this silent room. Lightning flickers in the storm's stern grasp.
Guttural thunder in the river's throat, echo of an old song.
Women, men, children march under torchlight, hoes and shovels
for weapons, the rusty blades, and bare feet dusty from the field.
They cross the river and sing, *Arise, ye slaves no more in thrall.*
Prisoners of starvation, their hungry mouths chew the bloody word,
Arise.

CROSSING

In Savoy Heights, two dark men stand, faced
off like twins, except one frowns with raised hand,
and the other laughs as he wrestles him sideways.
A sandy yard, a chinaberry tree, ripe fruit crushed
underfoot, sweet stench of a corpse. Underfoot.

Overhead, dried berries click, beads Beatrice had once
strung in a withered necklace, hung herself with the hope
that there would always be someone to look at her
chin raised, pale neck rising out of lace flounce.

Neighbors out on the porch to watch a bet get settled
never look as she drives by. The woman waters
snakeplants in tin cans, the woman ties on a flowered apron,
the man leans on a cedar railing, a clump of men wait
by the tar-shingled store. All stare at the two men, a story
she has no part in. No one stirs as she shifts into second
and a gauze of rain drops behind her. Curtained wall.

Picture window. Someone always outside to look in.
Skin of night. They needed eyes on what they had.

> White man rocking, white woman at the sewing machine,
> white girl reading, seemingly at peace. Mystery at home,
> domestic. She knew they were worth watching because
> the mother shouted, *Get a gun!* and the man leapt up,
> despite no gun in the house, and no one ever outside.

> The open window by her bed, perfumed gardenia.
> White skin bruised under the thumbs of rain. She waited
> for hands, brown, not too brown. Someone inside

to touch her. Someone outside, at the edge of night,
to watch the mouth poised over hers, to see her act.

In the storm, she drives toward a new home down creeks of streets. The car
wallows in the flood, loaded with boxes, old letters, the banjo
clock, the red glass buttons, the clay plates. Cold clay. Caul.

Skin of rain. No one looks, no one cares as she drives past.
The only eyes that see her stare back in the rearview glass.

The Gate

The gate is ajar in the iron-barred fence so she goes in.
A gate taller than she is. A slope of land between
a stack of apartments above, a railroad cut at the foot.

She goes in to smell something green, and the dirt in the rain,
the split dirt. One grave is fresh-turned, but some sit above ground,
like small cardboard boxes of ashes, with plastic toys on top,
and laminated snapshots nailed to a board at one end. Some
have red votive candles, burnt-out eyes. One has a bench
and a rosebush skeleton, planted by someone so something would
come back.

            This land has rows of names. She's never seen
so many words she's never heard out loud.

A freight train trundles past. Two, three times a day,
its weight comes to grind the wheels onto rails until they sing,
long wails, slowly answered. Like the rim of a crystal bowl
caught under circling fingers. Like something about to break.

UP NORTH

"They say that once a miner, always a miner. I don't know if that's so, but I do know that my father never followed any other trade. His sons never doubted that they would go down into the mines as soon as they got old enough.... [In 1932] we organized ... Unemployment Councils, and got rent and relief for a large number of families. We agitated endlessly for unemployment insurance.... The state held that ... my possession of Communist literature was enough to send me to the electric chair.... I spoke to the court and said ... 'You may succeed in killing one, two, even a score of working-class organizers. But you cannot kill the working class.'"
—*Angelo Herndon*

As she turns the corner, daylight begins to fail
and darkness falls down the bitter narrow
street, shadow valley between high-rise buildings
laddered with lights, lives clinging to the heights,
and she in the cleft between.
                                                    Like the night once,
on a mountain road running low around a hill,
she drove through a wilderness gap into a sudden
spangle of weightless lights. It was a city
high above, the steep galaxy of a mining town.

Her pa'd said he liked to work the mines,
cool even in summer. He named all the places
he ever worked, as his sweat fermented on his skin.
The mines were Dora, Yolande, Belle Ellen, Belle
Sumter. She'd wanted one named for her. Maybe there
was escape, maybe there would be a cave of rest.

Where she lives now, her rooms are suspended in air,
five floors up. Even at night there's no night there,
heaven turned to hell, the electric sweat of neon signs.
The city with no need of sun or moon to shine in it.

You have to be hard as stone to live in the city.
Sapphire, emerald, sardonyx. Topaz, jacinth, amethyst.
A jewel in a mail order catalog: International Assets,
Preferred Mines, economic turmoil, unusual low
prices. Dazzling splendor, beautiful gemstone.

You have to be hard enough to walk by people
who look up as you pass, country people who want
a face from home, but speak to you. You have
to be hard, or the hammer of their soft words
will break your heart like pile-driven stone.

If she's turning to stone, she'd rather be in the woods back home.
Wait for the seasons to turn, grind her to dust. Wait for
a deluge of rain to wash her, sparkling, back to dirt. She'd
rather be nothing but a lump of coal on a hill in dry bracken.

At nightfall, hands seize her. She's a stone foundation
for their fire, the boys out hunting for the night. Heat of pitch
pine and hickory sticks, and she begins to blaze.

Before dawn, the boys wake, then run when they see red
eyes staring from the ground, the very rocks on fire.

The coal seam smolders like old anger, and finally she falls
through, body of flame and smoke, tunneling underground.

First there is dead quiet. Then water dripping,
a louder shuffling. Lights bob like boats on water.
Then she sees the men come gleaming toward her.

Copper Quechua men plated with silver dust.
Black Sesotho men skinned with beaten gold.
Irish men polished jet-black from coal dust.
Colorado men, lead-poisoned, pallid, ghosts.

Stoop-shouldered, they stop to rub their swollen knees,
carbuncle-hard. They breathe out silver mist. They breathe
in dust. They cough to keep their lungs unpetrified.
They slowly turn to stone from inside out, stalagmite
arms up to pillar a roof that incessantly falls, feet mired
in a stream running black from the wastings of coal.

She creeps away through labyrinths, down wood ladders
slimed with mud. Far in front there is light. The clatter
of rain on tin roofs like a lunch pail rattling. A woman
singing, a woman screaming as she shakes a locked gate.
Scritch-scratching like hands digging up roots for food.

At the entrance, she looks down at her hands. At day's end
everyone comes out of Belle Ellen black. Black as soot,
black as pitch, black as the dried corpses once ground
to dust and drunk with brandy, elixir of immortal life,
bodies of slaves and prisoners salted and bound and laid
in the sun to petrify, skin turned bitumin, sold for medicine.

Black as the faces of striking miners hanging
at Mauch Chunk, as thousands stood silent to witness.

Later one shrouded in white spoke from the scaffold:
One day our silence will be stronger than the voices
you strangle today.

                                    She walks up the sloping track
into glitter, the city street. The sides of the city curve above.

People rush by, millions, picking their way through debris
piled up from Cerro Rico, the mountain of silver turned
inside out, Potosí become Huakajchi, the mountain that cried.

He was her guide. He lived in hell. Every day he thought
he was dead. Years after he's died, she thinks it's him stumbling
drunk through the subway turnstile. Just the two of them
on the platform. He asks her for money, pennies for passage:

In the nursing home, a palsied woman guards the door.
She asks: *Are you coming back?* Everyone in or out
must answer her. *Don't leave me here. Come back.*
Beatrice lies to get past her outstretched shaking hand.

Her father knows she's leaving him today. He waits.
His dying head turns and roams the air. One tear
slides from his right eye, rheumy clear regret.
What has he meant? His shouts at the TV asked for death,
the dogs set ravening. His way in the woods was delicate
wherever he stepped.

Before he takes her there,
he shows the snake's rattle in his desk drawer, stretched
out like a watch fob, a pocket charm to protect,
a souvenir of the biggest one he's killed yet. He calls
to her in the woods, *Look where you put your feet.*

Her favorite place is low, the watery creek branch,
sand rippled like snake tracks. His place is high, a stand
of longleaf pine. In that long hallway, light flashes
as his axe bites at a tree's distortions, rotted cankers,
excrescences. His gloved hands run rough up and down
the bark flanks. Her mouth fills with tincture of turpentine.
On the tree's face, teardrops of rosin harden and shine.

She remembers which way the bed faced. Climbing
up beside him. No touching, but excitement. Like getting on
a train and stories flash by. Him throwing tires like horseshoes
in Michigan, him wrestling alligators in a Florida swamp.
His words clack like wheels over rails, then he's snoring.

She thought they were going together. Left behind.
The one who waits, the one who's going nowhere
in the stuffy room, with his sweat, cigarettes, spittoon.
No way to tell her story.

                    He carries her on his back
          across the river. Sun sparkles under her feet,
          and the terror of what lies under. She climbs down
          to stand with him at the edge, where sandy ground
          gives way to water. His ruined land behind her,
          the failed sealed mouths of coal mines, the silver dollars
          like tarnished moons in men's hands on election night.

She knows she is leaving him today. She asks,
Will you die before I come back? He says he guesses so.
He sees her tears, he says, *Don't take it so hard.*

He promised his mother he'd come back. He never
promised her.

                    In the past they step to the edge of the river
                    and the water forgives.

He never promised to meet her
in the city, any one of the cities he stumbled through:

On foot in L.A. in 1931, looking for a job.
Left the trailer at dawn, walking. Sold cut flowers
on a corner, picked up golf balls at a driving range,
nickel a bucket. At the locked gates of the aircraft plant
daydreamed a flight above the city like a silver angel.
Asked for yard work at a house. The owner promises tomorrow.

He holds his hands out, and says, as if to a brother, a sister,
Don't you forget me.

Bone Day

On the way to the zoo, Beatrice passes discarded brick
mansions, once rich, worn by poor and poorer, then shed
like mangy coats or down-at-the-heel boots, tattered
houses made into funeral homes or office space
for owners who helicopter back and forth from their city
on weekends. On a Sunday night they might hover in
near the elephant yard, blow dust over bleached bones,
trees long since torn down by the animals out of boredom.

Inside, at cocktails, a birthday party for white Bengal cubs
or the gorilla's almost-human child, they toast rare species
they've paid to save. The silverback male, carved ebony face,
creeps out on a dead limb to piss. He fingers his ass, savors
a taste of shit, his only hors d'oeuvre of the day. Patrons hiss,
eyes askance, look somewhere he can't touch, the leafy roof
treed with parrots, the waterfall etched in electric wire.

By a tiny cage, a sign reads: *Baby, six weeks, removed.*
Maternal neglect. The female's matted breasts bulge with milk.

Outside the elephant swings her trunk, aimless bowed branch.
Her tone, inaudible, low to the ground, calls for others to come.
Snow and night fall on Beatrice walking in the wail of animals,

hapless, senseless. The big cats groan for the week's length, bone,
something to crack like the ice underfoot, some edge of escape.

Suppertime. The keepers wheelbarrow in boxes of greens and meat.
Hyenas grin over pig's heads skinned to a lard of bloody masks.
Teeth clacking, they chatter, *We'll grind your bones to make*
our bread. Only this moment do we caper captive for human gaze.

Inside the iron aviary, the condor, the vulture turn and track her.

> Unsmiling, they say, *We have spoken since before you began.*
> *You know what you know: Human cloth set from spider web,*
> *stone axe seen in beaver tooth. We are not myth,*
> *nor machines gone obsolete, and alone you are half a metaphor.*
> *One day, when some animal, smallest spore, opens its cell wall*
> *to embrace you, lying in your hut of earth, you'll rejoin us.*
>
> *What else are you to us? Learn before that judgment day the way*
> *the language of birds fledges your bone with the feather of words.*

Snake Eyes

At the corner wall, boys huddle and squat, playing
craps on school lunch hour. They bend and throw
and laugh. Mississippi marbles. Memphis dominoes.

Above, she cracks a window's ice edge open, to lean
outside. She can hear the dice rattling in their hands.

Shake the bones. What's left when you're done and gone.
Dirt. Filth. Husk of grain greases the millstone.
Gallows fruit and residue. The boss crapped out on me
and my money's flown.

                       Paper green as a leaf
changes hands. Trying to change their luck. Queen
Latifah talks to the neighborhood from a boombox, a beat
chant. One or two rock and cock response to her call.
In camouflage and hoods, disguised as death to fool death,
they snap their wrists, trying to twist the world on its axis
like a top. Someone shouts an oath to ward off snake eyes.

She has seen snakes writhe, eyes bleak with capture,
heathen devil held in the prison of their handlers' clutch.

First the preacher brought in death in a box.
Then he said, *Kneel down. Free your body*
from the world. The church was hot with shouts.
The sand they'd tracked in grated underfoot
as she slid back. He lifted up a rattlesnake
shaking its bony tail. Anointed with grace.

Trying to change his fate. She stood back,
unbeliever, visitor. She did not dance with death
coiled around her shoulders like a copper shawl.

Later she'd knelt at her window, praying for a sign.
Trying to change her life. It hadn't worked. No good.

There was always the moment, like what she's watching now:
The radio player walks catty-corner across the street
and gives a sign, unseen, unheard, but guessed at by her.
Like coins spilled from a pocket, the boys scatter.
One white policeman turns the corner, then another,
who taunts the stragglers, *Where's the game? Can't I
play? My money's good.*

                    The boys vanish up
and down the four ways, the crossed streets. Most go east.
East to the river. West to the city. North to the teachers.
South to the island. The four corners of the world meet
at the stoplight below her window. The cops lined up
the boys there last summer, and called them all thieves.
Every man-child in the neighborhood, six to sixteen.
No more fun and games. No music. No shouts.
Hands clasped behind heads, they stared at fifty years
shackled to jail or to a broom-leg job, and no
freedom key. No jubilation. No dancing in the streets.

The world's four winds meet at her corner. She has no choice
but to take her chance with the others. More than chance.
Go down in the one o'clock glare, car horns blaring, people
late for work. Cross to Selim's market for her bread
past the policeman on his beat. Unsmiling, refuse to bend her head.

The Shrine

At noon the veiled woman sat and wailed on the curb.
No one could get her to stop. The deli owner begged her
to take refuge. Beatrice could see his hands plead
in her language, the arc of deference. He promised the garden
behind the store, a sheltered wall, a chair in the sun.
She would not go. She would not shut a door on her grief.
Knees spread, hands writhed in her lap, she rocked in the street.

She is the unquiet mind from behind locked doors.
She is the suffering ocean broken through walls.
With her voice she makes herself an edifice of grief.

No one could stop her. When her son drove up in his Cadillac
to shove her in the front seat, she wailed, still alone. Incessant.
No intercession. No help from above.

The goddesses watched
from glass storefronts, the ones Beatrice sees as she walks.

In the window of Artículos Religiosos, Mary holds out
her hand. With no effort, her naked plaster feet crush
and spurn the serpent. In a blue cloak of sky, she is the queen,
heaven, earth, and hell. Her other hand spins a rose,
the red thread of blood she let down to pull up everyone.

Next to the laundromat, the Asian gift shop sells Kuan Yin.
Hers is the wish-bestowing gesture, the vow to cut
all fetters and knots. Her necklace is a golden vial of womb,
the boat that carries each soul across the suffering ocean.

Beatrice wishes she could pray to them:

Hum, Ma-ma,
Hum-ni, So-ha. Fold her hands in a *mudra* prayer,
fish swimming at the bottom of the pond, always muddy,
never dirty. Finger the garden of rosary beads. Count
the buds: *Mary, salve regina, how will you save me?*

She is six or seven, running to school. As she runs,
she cries. She crosses town square, past the stone soldier,
a church at each corner, the jail, and the judgment seat
at center. Something is lost. Something she has forgotten.

The grey clouds roll low, breakers from the ocean. Warm spit
on her cheek, rain mixed with tears. Something's been taken.

Mama is at work for money to save them. She can not ask her
for anything. By the store, a man yells and reaches out.
She thinks he knows her. He says, Wrong? *He wants to know*
more. Shame twists and breaks inside her. She runs on.
She knows her mother can not help her. She runs on alone.

On the crowded street, quitting time from work, a mother pushes
a child in a stroller, who looks up from deep shadows past
the shifting walls of people walking, past the bulk of buildings.
She reaches a hand from deep in her well, toward a silver coin,
a light she names and asks for, *Moon, moon, moon.*

Beatrice would pray for steady work, not to worry month
after month about the rent, the doctor's bills. On her walks
she has found no niche yet with a shrine to the women bent
over sewing machines or computer keyboards. No plaque
to the hands on fire with damaged nerves that no longer work.

The women of fury who every day hold up their hands like torches,
a warning to those who long for the broken paradise of their bodies.

First the fire engines shake the night, the red blare
outside on their usual route past her building. Then

later, lying in sleep's nest, in the boughs of darkness,
safe on the creaking highest floor of the old tenement,
she wakes to a whisper in her ear. The night supplicant
as intimate, as desperate in request as a lover's *please*.

His staccato whisper raps on her neighbor's door. *It's me.*
From the hallway the whisper slides to her pillow. *Fuego.*
A trickle of sound like sand, a tired dry desire. *We lost
everything.* He talks to the ear of darkness, to the eye
of silence. *Tenemos nada. Nada.*

                              She hears a hinge creak,
the jaws of measured speech. Then her room is emptied of
everything except what he has brought and left behind:
how the flames came close enough to lick her hand.

Next morning, under her window, the corner has a new rumor:
Fire was set to smoke the tenants out, the wild bees honeycombed
in a house worth twice what it cost. Enough smoke, they drop,
stunned, and get swept away like dirt clods out the door.

Summer mornings she looked out the back window
from her grandma's house. The women stood shifting
from foot to foot in the dirt, avoiding the eddies of smoke
from their low fires.

                              The women, hired to clean
and do the wash, were boiling clothes in black iron pots.
Hominy lye soap so strong and mean, it would skin your hands,
her grandma said, so the sheets could be clean from every sin,
washed free, whiter than, whiter than, snow.

                                                    The women
stood by their kettles. They talked. They laughed. Every so often
they poked a stick at what was seething there. It could have been
anything, brain, entrails, skin. It could have been the secret of life.

They hooked the clothes out with their sticks, and wrung them
dry as a chicken's neck. They wrung them until grief
fell in scalding drops back into the pot, and boiled again.

Early morning means Beatrice goes down and around the corner
to fetch drinking water. Half the women of the world are doing
the same but walking further, while she pays a dollar fifty a gallon.

A door opens at the corner's triangle. A woman is sweeping
crumbs of fire into the street. Inside there is clapping, there is
a song. At the threshold's altar Beatrice sees hands that flash fire.
Then the door slams shut.

                              In grief she's rubbed her hands
together, hard, harder, like dry sticks of wood. Now anger
has smoldered a long time. What is she to do?

                                        Days she goes
to see movies at the mall, to sit alone with her neighbors,
watching disaster strike luxury shops in Beverly Hills,

a fire of molten lava pave the streets. Or skyscrapers
in New York explode into infernal bloom. Hell incinerates
the landlords who scoffed at warnings. The bad guys burn.

At night in bed she listens as sirens split the sleeping world
into homeless and the rest. She begins a mental list of what
she would try to save. She could pack a bag with photographs
and her poems, and keep it between her bed and the fire escape,
like a scuttle of hot coals to lug from place to place.

                                              Tinder
       blazes up, light flickers over mouths shut on the word
       nothing.

The Ferry

"You know, we ain't dumb, even if we are poor. We need jobs. We need food. We need houses. But even with the poverty program we ain't got nothin but needs. That's why we was pulled off that building that wasn't being used for anything. We is ignored by the government. The thing about property upset them, but the things about poor people don't. So there's no way out but to begin your own beginning, whatever way you can. So far as I'm concerned, that's all I got to say about the past."
—*Mae Lawrence*

Today, she tells the woman close beside her, *I saw a man*
in the thicket by the river bridge.

                                 She saw him because it rained
hard and he moved slow. He stepped from his invisible cloak,
water sewn seamless by needles of rain, and unfolded
a cardboard box, propped it against a gumtree, sat casual
like the way she adjusts a pillow in her living room. Then she looked
in the wasteland at what was trash. Corrugated tin bent
into shelter lean-tos, and there was one webbed string tent,
a woven home beside a pile of blue-green jewels, bottles.

Where the river sludged with mud, tires, a shopping cart,
she could see a footpath worn down through stinging nettles,
to the stone road across the stream at a fording place.

And when she saw this, the bridge shook under her.

                                      Some day,
maybe, she says, *I'll take you home to see my river.*

In summer, a place of thunder, dry dirt into sudden water,
and the dead ruts of loggers' roads sparkle with quartz.
In winter, sycamore trees lean upstream, white branches,
bones picked clean, the roost where a dozen buzzards gather.
Downstream, an island from backwash of sand. Seems a place
where nothing's ever happened. But there was a ferry once.

On the black river, blurred light, a lantern on the dock.
A white woman at the winch chooses who will cross. Once
she cut the cables and lost the boat, a year's money, to keep out
the soldiers who'd come to free the slaves she carried,
the ones who tilled the bottom land.

On the slurried bank,
a secret fire always blazes. Someone, no coin for passage,
waits for low water and massed night shadows to wade in.
Someone's voice always foams, seething, in the rapids.

I'll never find my girl Phebe again. Shoes drug me,
foot sore, down.

Farewell, Cahawba, Oka Aba.
Farewell, Haysoppy.

We want to stay, they make us leave.
We want to leave, they make us stay on no land for all.

It was never her river, sold before she knew it. Yet it was hers.
How could she leave it? The blue shining darters, the lily stars.
Walnut meat sweet inside a thick-shelled skull, leaves crushed
to bitter musk. Creek mouthing below the river bend. But a house
forted in on the land could not make it hers.

Now limestone
grey bluffs, cenotaphs, mark the passing of those who tried
to buy. And money still drives down from the city, inexorable, slow,
a bulldozer scraping choice suburban plots from the scenic bank.
An old man in another state writes to ask if five cedars planted
small are living yet? Spared by a marring hand? Though the old tree's
gone, brought down when he sold his place, and the railroad graded.

Meanwhile, in this declivity, wedged between two ridges, the trees
wait for the people who know them by sight, each winter silhouette
familiar as a sister's height, her handprint. The people who walk
to pick up lightwood for their fire, or pine needles for baskets.

The ones who said: *If the dead could have counted, the land never
would have been sold, but, alas, though they stood around, and their tears
came in raindrops, they could not be seen, and the white man's plough
furrowed up their bones.*

Someday, she says to the woman,
*I'll take you to see my river, and the house my people built
fallen in on its foundation.*

Cellar gaping like a grave draped
in creeper and catbriar, timber frame stripped sure as the bone-
pickers unraveled flesh from corpse.
Now I have no home.

On the winter river, the ferry woman would not have carried them,
with their voice of lost souls, of owls mating deep in the night,
cries cracking like trees falling,   *hoohoo-hoohoo   hoohoo-hoohoo-aw.*

The bed trembles like a bridge falling, her
face down, spread, dead woman's float. Then over
at the other's hand, laving, not saving her, but
a meeting of waters, hidden shoals. The boat
of her legs, a vee of white, opens, waits.

In rain and street light, on the concrete ledge of the bridge, graffiti
glows orange, words phosphorescent as a campfire, near the man
who leans back against a tree's damp bed. The words say,
We love you Manuel. They say, *Cathrine Fire here today.*

They say, *We are crossing here, this bridge our only land.*

The Great Migration

"...paid for at a price which literally staggers humanity. Imperialism, the exploitation of colored labor throughout the world, thrives upon the approval of the United States, and the United States gives that approval because of the South."
—*W. E. B. Du Bois*

The third question in Spanish class is: *¿De dónde eres tú?*
She'd come for brand-new words: *las flores rojas, el puente.*
To have words like *crema de leche* on her tongue at least
for a few weeks before tasting the bitter syllables of their history.

How to begin with the young woman next to her asking: *Where?*
Young enough to be her daughter but—

> *The place where you were one of five half-naked children*
> *playing in the dirt under a porch. There was a yellow dog.*
> *The place where I was a white girl sitting in a dusty car*
> *with the window rolled down, looking at you. No word*
> *to share. That place. That place.*

She says, *Del Sur.*
The girl replies: *We moved up here when I was eight.*
Until last year every dream I had happened there.
I take my daughter down to see my aunts. She's four.
Back home she can take her shoes off. The ground's not
strewn with glass, like here. The dirt's clean, at least.
Do you have folks, back home?

From class to home
she tries out her lessons. At the bus stop bench, she sat next to
a man who hated spring, its thunderhead clouds, its green-
leafed rain. At home, he said, there was only sun. In the north

in Chile, rain was somewhere else, not falling everywhere
like sadness here. He'd not been back in twenty years.

There was him, and the man who hated the cold and the brick factory
and the one room with fifteen people he couldn't remember. He began
to walk back to Guatemala. Police picked him up in Texas.
No soles to the bottom of his shoes. Police stopped him in Mexico.
Three thousand miles in four months. He'd done it before. His compass
was walk south, toward warmth, you come to home before the war.

At home there was a dirt track by the paved road, worn down
through pink sundrops and fox grass, an emphatic sentence
written by people walking north to work.

                                    Books called it
The Great Migration, but people are not birds. They have in common
only flight. Now, in the city night, they dream they're caught
in a cloud of dust and grit, looking down at land being shoveled,
furrowed, or burned by huge machines. In the daylight they stand
in line at the post office and buy money orders to send home.

        Beatrice is there to collect a package from her mother. This time
        she's sent onions grown in sandy soil. She says they are sweeter
        than apples, that one will feed a crowd, that they have no bitterness.

                At home their neighbor said: *I can tell any county I'm in
                just by smelling the dirt.*

                                    Beatrice puts aside five
        onion globes shining yellow as lamplight, like the old kerosene
        lamp they set in the kitchen for emergencies. She'll give
        them to the woman who sits by her in Spanish class, the one
        young as a daughter, the one she'd never have known at home.

Trash

That day the most beautiful thing she saw was pigeons.
Neatly dressed in grey and silver stripes, or snuff brown,
like office workers, except the shocking ascot, the neck
oilslick green and purple, the finicky pink naked feet.

Walking barefoot in broken glass and crushed paper cups,
what are the pigeons learning? Assiduously searching through
the scattered trash of human lives, they startle Beatrice.
She's used to them flying by like windblown plastic bags.

Now she's fixed by one scavenger eye, coy,
shy, trash with consciousness. The bird cocks its head
sideways, feminine wile, a friend's attention. Suddenly

she's standing in a city peopled by birds, their hub-bub
conversation, and their wheeling flight toward home, the rock
cliffs of skyscraper and church steeple, each cranny and nook
they remember from when they nested there, rockdove
high above the river in the granite palisades, long before
convenient niche apartments were built for them by men.

Face damp on a lover's thigh and scratchy
pubic hair, she sighs in the wet dirt smell,
steam rising from hot ground and underbrush,
the hollow place, bottom of the hill, where
cars stopped for it seemed no reason, until
one day she saw a young thin woman digging up
the yellow-brown clay, crumbly as cornmeal
put in a paper sack. She'd never tried the dirt
but thought the woman had a power she did not,
tasting that mysterious meal late at night.

Now Beatrice envied no other's power, licking
acrid delicate salt from her lips. Not anymore,
as she lay back pliant in another's steady hand,
thou-art-the-potter-I-am-the-clay. Surrender.
Oh yes, the way she'd never done in church.

Closest then she'd ever come was in the shed
cool as a scooped-out cave, beside a dirt road
miles from nowhere, in a world that went on with
no help from her, even Ed could not do a thing
when the wild turkey hen and her chicks crossed by
but wish for his gun. The world went on around.
Breathe, rot, eat and be eaten, regardless.

In the shed, grey rows of pots dripped wet, just born,
some small as a hand, some thick through the body.
When the potter let her kick the board, the wheel spun
heavy as a car on muddy ground, the squat clay lump
sliding in her hand. The slightest touch changed

everything. Thumb, hooked as if to peel an orange
at the navel, suddenly would plumb the earth's core.
Her fingers laid mountains low into glistening bowls.

Soon they'd breakfast off plates lifted whole from that place.
She'd set the table with a thump, ready for the morning news,
the next story about women like her, the same question,
What made you the way you are?

                      She'd say straightfaced it was
the dirt she ate.

                And in the coming night she'd shiver.
In the candle's flame the blue eye of a waiting kiln. Touch
scorches her breasts, her belly fattened with desire. The other
woman, panting, digs between her legs. Candle shadows
eat the wall, nether light swallows up the fire.

Sweat glazes her pale skin, done, undone by one touch
and terror, never knowing whether what will come will be
surrender, the tongue's flame in the furnace of the mouth.

"Whenever my mother, Matilde Rodríguez Torres, was asked about her
work as a seamstress in the garment factories of Manhattan, she would
sigh and say: '¡En la aguja y el pedal, eché la hiel!' ['Into the needle and
the pedal I poured my bitterness!']. . . . The story of my mother is one
of many stories that make up the history of Puerto Rican garment
workers in America in the twentieth century. . . . the first in the [New
York] area to experience on a large scale the negative consequences of
the production and labor market changes that resulted from the
globalization of the industry after the 1960s."
—*Altagracia Ortiz*

The Remnant Shop

In and out the window the red silk curtain fluttered,
breathed in with spring air, some hope of beginning again, out
with music, jazz, someone alive on the third floor. Not alone.
The bones of music dancing in the four walls of the blues.

She passes by the house and begins to plot. What costume, what
dress, what fabric, felted, knotted, braided, twisted,
intaglio printed, damask woven, what roving thread
would clothe her tonight? At the shop on Paterson Street she stops
to muss the remnants with her hand, whisking and tossing, silk
spilling through her fingers like water down a causeway, spill-
way. Three yards of silk tagged at thirty-nine fifty.

Thirteen dollars a yard, four dollars a foot, why she
didn't make that an hour when she worked at the plant. Her foot
stamped and stepped every two seconds, that's thirty times
a minute, and eighteen hundred times an hour and fourteen
thousand four hundred times a day. How many miles
a day? But you can't go far on just one foot. Hobbled.

She sat outside at noon, alone, with the other women.
They sat in the shadow of the picnic shelter. The white women.
The Black women ate elsewhere. (Where?) So did the men,
the white men. No Black men allowed. The women sat outside
in the heat and said it was hotter than Shadrach's furnace. Hard to
breathe. Soon the inside of the plant seemed inviting, air-
conditioned. Like the icehouse. *Or the funeral home!* said someone.
No other cool place. The creek, spring fed, but you did that as a kid.

So she ate her sandwich in five minutes, and read the rest
of the half hour. She sat apart from the others, awkward, the book
open on her lap, the light glaring on the page as she read
Greek history. The names of the cities at war were beautiful
to her like no sound she'd heard except in the Bible, a sound
that opened a crack, a fracture, a fissure, in the parking lot
too hot to walk on, in the red dirt field, in the thick-walled
brick garment plant. She was going to slip through, if she could
keep reading and not hear what the women were saying.

> *The swollen belly. Ran away by the river. The church elders*
> *said don't never come back. The swollen belly. Everyone*
> *knew he used to teach Sunday school. Everyone*
> *knew what she had done. Everyone knew. Everyone.*

Her head down, eyes on the page. The men with shields.
The red silk sails. The women at home weaving. Her head
down, and next summer the same, except on the line. Her hand
smoothed the fabric. This way, that way. Do the pieces match?
She touched the plush pile. She roughed the nap to see which way
was against the grain. She talked to no one about loneliness,
the machinery, people every day with hands like levers. Her foot

a lever that closed the circuit, weight pressed against
pure resistance, until an electric thread lock-stitched.
She held up dissected cloth and matched the halves and made
them whole. At the end of summer, she walked out of the silence
that rings when the buzzer sounds, and everyone switches off
her machine and leaves.

           In high school, economics was required
but she took music, and anyway no one would have taught her what
she's learned since about the road from Ulaanbataar to Samarqand,
through Lyon and across the ocean.

           The silk houses trembled
like water in the desert wind. The women hung their work
on mud walls, *ikat* eyes, red blue yellow, staring
into the sun.

           In the Czar's plantations, fields of cotton lay
like snow blighting wheat and cabbages, while the peasants smashed
the sluice gates at the irrigation ditches.

           On Croix-Rousse hill
austere buildings grew taller. Inside, the workers stood
in waterfalls of thread, jacquards overhead, weaving brocade.
They shouted, *Vivre en travaillant, mourir en combattant!*
struck the machines, and poured through their hidden passageways.

She shakes out folds of fabric that snap like laundry in the wind,
skirts and pants on the fire escape line, out a tenement window
like where she lives now at the edge of palisaded rock, the fracture,

where the creeks and rivers drop down to a greater river, and the old
factories rise up as office buildings bright with flags
written over with new corporate logos, flapping in the breeze

        where in 1913 the company sheriff tried to make
        the strikers fly the U.S. flag when they marched. But they
        refused. One held up his hand and said: *We dyed the thread,*
        we spun the thread, we wove the cloth that made the flag.
        We dyed the thread, with our very hands. This is my flag!

        Holding up his red red hand, scorched sores, caustic eyes.

The sanguine curtains breathing in and out, imbued with meaning
 by a human hand.

           On her way home, every brick of the building
she stands in front of is clay baked and set in place
by someone who didn't own the land, the house, or maybe
even the trowel in his hand. The asphalt shingles on the roof—
someone pressed the felt, tarred and sprinkled it with sparkling
gravel someone broke from rock like that beneath her feet.
Someone set out the blue plastic pots, intending yellow
princess feathers. Unsealed the seeds that someone had gathered
into packets.

        Each person walking by is clothed in radiance
wrought by unseen hands, in the shoelaces knotted firmly
on the schoolchildren's feet, in the books they carry. Inside
are the math problems and history lessons, and poems made
by someone like her, standing on the street in morning rush hour.

Someone raised up by a woman told to keep the two of them
separate, never drink water from the same cup, the woman
who took Beatrice on her lap as the light faded, and held her
in the twilight, in the hard touch of her callused fingers.

The woman whose first job as a girl was to sew men's shirts.
She fastened on pearl buttons in a little factory down near Nanih Waiya.

Cost and Use

Velvet slippers, one on the sidewalk, the other, debris
in a yard. A vanished woman, split in two by mesh fence.
At midnight, she walked barefoot. At midday, a man
faces the Latin Chef window. He reads the menu, his eyes

eat each item. His hands spread his wallet, his eyes
count each dollar. In one history, this is the end.
In another, a beginning. Along the block, people tend
their yards. Beatrice can see who remembers the country, crammed

into buckets of dirt, cantilevered on old boards, farmed
with okra, basil, tomatoes, aloe, cilantro, blue corn,
bitter melon. Twine takes bean vines up into a crown,
a shawl of shade. How frightened she was when she moved

into the four rooms, no yard, no way to grow her food.
To eat she always has to sell something. Her deft hands,
like women who paint roses by the hour, fancy designs
flowering on the edge of plates they can't afford to buy.

Or words that she strings together, ideas of things, dry
fertile seeds made by the sunflowers now turning their heads
in an arc of light in the yard beside her:

                                    Between thought and deed,
she is rife with words, enough and not worth a penny a pound.

But they answer a need sharp as hunger and thirst. They feed the doubt
that gnaws on habit and the past. They pay for the act that breaks free.

Men flirt in the silvered mirror, eyelids, shadow-
wings. The dance-floor red-blue spotlights shine hot
as lantern glow. At showtime, Beatrice works to know
who is woman. The pumping dancer, gripped naked
by spandex at the crotch, could she hide a resting cock?
Her breasts insist on homage, thrust at every mouth.
Beatrice holds up crisp dollars, twist into cleft, sweat,
is rewarded by a haughty look: *I deserve everything I get.*
A lady with beaded breasts caught under bronze net
lip syncs a torch song, languid hand full of taxi money
to carry her, still dancing, lanky legs, past boys
idling outside, a fist of baseball bats, to prove her man.

A crowd circles the stage. Dark and pale faces blaze
above what runs fiery toward them, like kerosene spilled
from a kicked-over lantern. The spirit goes this way
and that, like rainwater shifts on a clay dance ground,
stepping from one sunken footprint to another. She watches
their mouths, the people about to kneel and drink their desire.
They will lick burning water from the dirt. They will rise up
bold in a body they have never worn.
                                    The emcee jokes:
Get to be as old as me, have to decide if you're a he or she,
scolds her niece-nephew, her nephew-niece, which is Mawu,
which Lisa? One clanks keys from a cinched fighter's belt,
the other flutters hands and lashes.

                            The unsmiling woman
at her elbow asks Beatrice sideways, *What kind of woman
are you? Stand here. Answer.* Rearing proud head, she shies

at touch, a hand on her rough starched shirt. Yet her voice leads, low, whispering, *Answer me and live.*

Wanting to taste
her scarred path, to trace with tongue each danger passed.

To meet at a forgotten crossroads, a makeshift altar,
a pile of stones, plastic roses, red ribbon, a sign
with illegible words from a god once there. To kneel and lick
her palm, scraped raw, shoved down on stones. To walk on,
their feet raising dust in the road.
                                    To enter the lean-to
house and lie down as night rises, fog billowing like smoke
up from the fields. Inside, a fire, the bloody shirt stripped off.

To lie under her, to become the place both are going,
a rhythm like oars in water. The winter begun outside.
The snakes asleep. None to lick her ears so she could
hear an answer, none waiting to steal her words.

On her own
about how to answer, she waits for the unknown woman to ascend
through smoke, past the grinning bouncer, the vending machine.
She waits for her boot clack on the stair, old sound of desire.

Beatrice waits for the woman with eyes that say, *Come with me.*
Into the rain-streaked street of night, the yellow leaves fallen
like golden scars on black asphalt, they walk out their answer
to the riddle, the woman who is not a man, the woman who is not
a woman, following the yellow drift like fire around the corner.

"SHADES"

Some of the details in this poem are drawn from a narrative written by Olaudah Equiano (1745–1797), who was born into the Ibo people in what is now modern Nigeria. He was kidnapped and sold into slavery when he was eleven years old. He survived the Middle Passage, the journey of abducted Africans in slavers' ships across the Atlantic to the Americas. From the mid 1400s to the mid 1800s, the international slave trade claimed the lives of untold millions of African peoples. Equiano, also known as Gustavus Vassa, was the first native African and former slave to write the story of his life without a white editor or ghostwriter. See *The Interesting Narrative and Other Writings*, ed. Vincent Carretta (1789; rpt. New York: Penguin, 1995); the epigraph is from pp. 62–63.

"CENTRAL PRISON"

Velma Barfield of North Carolina was the first woman executed in the United States after the death penalty was reinstated in 1976; two other women have been executed since. A report on the death penalty in the United States, released in 1996 by the International Commission of Jurists, shows that African-American men made up 40 percent of the people executed in the United States between 1973 and 1995. African Americans comprise about 13 percent of the U.S. population. See Teresa Gutierrez, "Barbaric Execution," April 3, 1997, on Workers World <www.workers.org>.

"BUST OF MARTHA MITCHELL TO BE UNVEILED"

Martha Mitchell (1918–1976), born in Arkansas, was married to John Mitchell, Attorney General for U.S. President Richard M. Nixon. Her husband resigned in 1972 to head the Committee for the Re-Election of the President, later linked to the Republican operatives who were hired to commit the Watergate burglary. Mitchell claimed that she had been forcibly prevented from speaking out about the criminal involvement of high-ranking Nixon administration officials in undisclosed wrongdoing. She was later committed to a mental institution.

"You shall know the Truth and the Truth shall make you free": John 8:32 in the King James Bible.

"After the iron sound": In May 1963, Children's Marches took place in Birmingham, Alabama, as part of a larger initiative for African-American civil rights. Police dogs and high-power water from fire department hoses were used against the children, and two thousand were arrested. In June 1963, after almost ten years of right-wing bombings and terrorist activity organized by the white political and economic power structure against the civil rights movement, a bomb exploded on a Sunday morning at the Sixteenth Street Baptist Church in Birmingham. Killed were four African-American girls: Denise McNair, age eleven, Addie Mae Collins, age fourteen, Carole Robertson, age fourteen, and Cynthia Wesley, age fourteen. In 1977, Robert Chambliss, a member of a Ku Klux Klan group known as the "Cahaba Boys," was finally convicted for the bombing, in part based on the testimony of his niece, Elizabeth H. Cobbs. In 1989, Cobbs, a female-to-male transsexual, transitioned to an identity as Petric Smith. See Elizabeth H. Cobbs/Petric J. Smith, *Long Time Coming* (Birmingham, Ala.: Crane Hill, 1994).

"RED STRING"

Epigraph from Ida B. Wells-Barnett, *Crusade for Justice: An Autobiography of Ida B. Wells*, ed. Alfreda M. Duster (Chicago: University of Chicago Press, 1970), pp. 70–71. Wells-Barnett (1862–1931) was born in Holly Springs, Mississippi, to enslaved parents. She became a journalist and newspaper publisher in Memphis. Her organizing began when three African-American men, all personally known to her, were lynched in 1892.

"They took my boy": The voices in this poem are fragments of the testimony of witnesses recorded in *Report of the Joint Select Committee to Inquire into the Condition of Affairs in the Late Insurrectionary States: 42nd Congress, 2nd Session* (Washington, D.C.: Government Printing Office, 1872), vols. 8–10. In this record of repressive violence in the South following the end of the Civil War in 1865, freed slaves and white radical Republicans provided eyewitness accounts of the murders, rapes, floggings, and intimidation carried out by paramilitary groups like the Ku Klux Klan, who were loyal to, and organized by, the financial interests of the former Confederate States. In 1915, the second Ku Klux Klan, organized on a national basis, targeted Blacks, Jews, immigrants, Catholics, trade unionists, communists, and sexually independent women. The first lynching victim of the revived Klan was Leo Frank, a Jew accused of raping a white woman in Atlanta. This revived Klan included mayors, governors, U.S. congressmen, and at least one future U.S. Supreme Court Justice, Hugo Black.

Resistance to these waves of violence was extensive and varied, and included the antilynching campaign of Ida B. Wells-Barnett.

"A COLD NOT THE OPPOSITE OF LIFE"

Epigraph from Harry Haywood, "Shadow of the Plantation," from *Negro Liberation* (1948), rpt. in *Black on White: Black Writers on What It Means to Be White*, ed. David R. Roediger (New York: Schocken, 1998), p. 127. Haywood (1898–1985) was an African-American organizer and theorist whose autobiography was titled *Black Bolshevik* (1978).

"Beatrice had facts about her from a book": This tenant farm woman, who speaks later in the poem, is a composite of the many women who appear in Margaret Jarman Hagood's *Mothers of the South: Portraiture of the White Tenant Farm Woman* (1939; rpt. New York: W. W. Norton, 1977). In the late nineteenth and early twentieth centuries, landowners of antebellum Southern plantation acreage arranged cultivation of their holdings through share tenancy and sharecropping. In tenancy, farmers usually owned mules or equipment. Their portion of the crop might be two-thirds to three-fourths, less the cost (inflated by usurious interest) of fertilizer, seed, food, and clothing that had been advanced from the plantation commissary or a local store. In sharecropping, farmers usually brought only their labor to the field, and received no more than half the crop, less the cost with interest of materials advanced for their subsistence. By 1930, tenancy had increased steadily as more and more independent farmers lost their land; in that year nearly half the Southern farm population were tenant and sharecropping families. See "Sharecropping and Tenancy," in *Encyclopedia of Southern Culture*, ed. Charles Reagan Wilson and William Ferris (Chapel Hill, N.C.: University of North Carolina Press, 1989).

"STRANGE FLESH"

"She'd tried to be not herself": Details about Marie Curie are from the biography by her daughter, Eve Curie, *Madame Curie: A Biography* (Garden City, N.Y.: Doubleday, 1937). Born in Poland in 1867, Marie Curie died in France in 1934. She was the first person to win two Nobel Prizes, the first in 1903 for the discovery of radioactivity with her husband and colleague, Pierre, and the second in 1911 for the isolation of radium.

"A little white man nodded through the crowd": In 1942, J. Robert Oppenheimer was appointed director of the laboratory in Los Alamos, New

Mexico, that designed and constructed the first atomic bomb. He also headed the scientific panel that recommended U.S. use of this bomb in its war with Japan. On August 6 and 9, 1945, the U.S. government bombed Hiroshima and Nagasaki in the first and, until this day, only use of a nuclear bomb. See Hiroshima <www.lclark.edu/~history/HIROSHIMA/index.html>.

"How those who know as beasts": Jude, verses 7 and 8, in the King James Bible.

"THE POSSUM EATS OUT OF THE GRAVEYARD"

Epigraph from Ruby Bates, qtd. in James Goodman, *Stories of Scottsboro: The Rape Case That Shocked 1930s America and Revived the Struggle for Equality* (New York: Pantheon, 1994), p. 198. Bates spoke these words in 1933 before a crowd of five thousand in Baltimore. In March 1931, after hearing of a fight between Black and white youths on a freight train in northern Alabama, a sheriff's posse stopped the train. Nine young African-American men were arrested, following an accusation of rape from Bates and Victoria Price, two young white women. Bates and Price were mill workers who were also riding the rails looking for jobs. The youths were Olen Montgomery, Clarence Norris, Haywood Patterson, Ozie Powell, Willie Roberson, Charley Weems, Eugene Williams, Andrew Wright, and Roy Wright, aged twelve to twenty. They were jailed in Scottsboro, the county seat. Slightly over two weeks later, eight of them had been tried and sentenced to death. National and international outrage over their sentence focused on the flimsy evidence of rape, and on the fact that violence against African-American men in the late nineteenth and early twentieth centuries had often been justified as "the protection of white woman-hood." The International Labor Defense, the legal affiliate of the Communist Party-U.S.A., defended the Scottsboro Nine on appeal. There were seven retrials and two landmark Supreme Court decisions in the case (*Powell v. Alabama*, 287 U.S. 56, and *Norris v. Alabama*, 294 U.S. 599). The young men were never acquitted; they spent from six to nineteen years in jail. In the summer of 1947, Haywood Patterson escaped from Kilby Prison after saying to a friend, "I'm giving myself a pardon"; he later wrote *Scottsboro Boy* (Garden City, N.Y.: Doubleday and Company, 1950). A detailed account of these political and legal struggles can be found in Dan Carter, *Scottsboro: A Tragedy of the American South* (1969; rpt. New York: Oxford University Press, 1976).

"The fishy smell, Bahia Medía Luna": Half Moon Bay in Vieques, Puerto Rico.

"Down to the forbidden beach": Puerto Rico, occupied and colonized at the beginning of the 1500s by Spain, was shifted by the mid 1600s from a mining economy to an agricultural economy based on sugar cane cultivation. The island became part of a triangle of trade in which slave ships, financed by local investors in Europe or the United States, sailed to Africa to kidnap or buy human beings, then to the Caribbean or the most southern states of the United States to sell their cargoes of workers destined for the plantations. The ships were then loaded with sugar, molasses, or rum produced from processing cane, and sailed on to further earn rich profits for the investors. After 1898, when the United States seized the island as a colony, American corporate capitalists poured in huge investments to control and expand the sugar industry. See Arturo Morales Carrión, *Puerto Rico: A Political and Cultural History* (New York: W. W. Norton, 1983).

"The bulldozer grinds": On Vieques, one of the four main islands of Puerto Rico, two-thirds of the island has been expropriated by the U.S. government since the beginning of World War II. These holdings have become a naval base, a staging area for U.S. military interventions in the Caribbean, and the site of the Atlantic Fleet Weapons Range. By 1950, ships firing from sea dropped an average of 3,400 bombs a month on the island and the waters around it. Vieques residents who subsisted by fishing have organized flotillas of protest in target areas. See Ronald Fernandez, *Prisoners of Colonialism: The Struggle for Justice in Puerto Rico* (Monroe, Maine: Common Courage Press, 1994).

"AT DEEP MIDNIGHT"

Epigraph from the complete text of Cheryl Harris's "Whiteness as Property" appeared in the 1993 *Harvard Law Review*. The quote here is from an excerpt of that article in *Black on White,* ed. Roediger, p. 103.

"THE ROAD TO SELMA"

Epigraph from B. J. Simms, qtd. in *The Walking City: The Montgomery Bus Boycott, 1955–1956,* ed. David J. Garrow (Brooklyn: Carlson Publishing, 1989), p. 579.

"Reeb, Liuzzo, Jimmie Lee Jackson": Early in 1965, civil rights activists organized in and around Selma, Alabama, to protest discriminatory voter registration practices aimed at preventing African-American citizens from casting ballots in any election. The organizing in Selma continued a wave of civil rights protest that had gathered momentum with the Montgomery bus boycott, initiated by Beulah Johnson, Rosa Parks, and other African-American women of the community in 1955. During the organizing in Selma, Jimmie Lee Jackson, one of the African-American voter registration workers, was shot and killed by a state trooper. A nonviolent march to Montgomery was organized to protest his death. On March 7, about five hundred demonstrators walked out of Selma and crossed the bridge over the Alabama River. They were set upon by local and state police with clubs, beaten, teargassed, and driven back into town. In a later incident, a white Unitarian minister, James Reeb, was beaten and died. On March 15, President Lyndon Johnson called upon a joint session of Congress to pass a voting rights bill. On March 21, another Selma-to-Montgomery march began. About 3,200 people, including Dr. Martin Luther King Jr., walked twelve miles a day, camped at night, and reached Montgomery four days later, where about forty thousand people rallied. On the evening of that day, Viola Liuzzo, a civil rights worker, was driving marchers home through Lowndes County when she was shot and killed by a group of white men. The legal defense for these men was subsequently paid for by the United Klans of America. In August, the U.S. Congress passed the Voting Rights Act of 1965. See the entry for 1965 in Peter M. Bergman and Mort N. Bergman, *The Chronological History of the Negro in America* (New York: NAL/Mentor, 1969), and Patsy Sims, *The Klan* (New York: Stein and Day, 1978).

"We jumped rope": The voices in this poem are, in part, echoes and fragments of the voices of the African-American people interviewed by John Livingston Gwaltney for *Drylongso: A Self Portrait of Black America* (New York: W. W. Norton, 1981).

"The road to Snow Hill": William J. Edwards, born in 1868 to former slaves and raised by his grandmother, studied at Tuskegee Institute under Booker T. Washington. In 1893, he returned home to Snow Hill in Wilcox County, south of Selma, and established Snow Hill Normal and Industrial Institute. The school was founded on Washington's model of industrial education as a means for African Americans in the South to escape from sharecropping into self-employment and land ownership. The institute continues today as Springtree/Snow Hill Institute for the Performing Arts under the direction of Edwards's granddaughter, Consuela Lee. See William James Edwards, *Twenty-five Years in the Black Belt* (Tuscaloosa: University of Alabama Press, 1993), and Springtree/ Snow Hill at <www.auburn.edu/~perrirw/snow.html>.

"The road to Camp Hill": Ralph Gray was born in 1878, the grandson of an African-American state legislator during Reconstruction. Gray became a farmer in Tallapoosa County, Alabama, east of Selma. In 1929, with cotton prices and the stock market collapsing, poor farmers were pushed deeper into debt and began to organize throughout the South. In 1931, Gray joined the Communist Party-U.S.A. and started building the Croppers' and Farm Workers' Union. The CFWU had won a few small victories when landlords retaliated. Vigilantes deputized by the county sheriff raided a union meeting where Gray was standing armed guard. In the ensuing gun battle, they shot and eventually killed Gray. Despite severe antiunion violence, organizing continued in Tallapoosa and other counties, such as Lee and Lowndes. In 1935, a strike of cotton pickers more than doubled wages. See Robin D. G. Kelley, *Hammer and Hoe: Alabama Communists During the Great Depression* (Chapel Hill, N.C.: University of North Carolina Press, 1990).

"White rooster. Black panther": In 1965, the Student Nonviolent Coordinating Committee (SNCC), under the leadership of Stokely Carmichael (later Kwame Toure), came to Lowndes County to launch a voter registration drive, and held joint meetings with a local church-based group. The meetings were attended by an older generation of farmers who came armed and recalled the union battles of the 1930s. The organization that resulted, the Lowndes County Freedom Organization, took as its emblem the black panther. In 1966, when Huey P. Newton and Bobby Seale founded the Black Panther Party in Oakland, California, they named it after the LCFO's panther. That spring, the LFCO ran African-American candidates for office in Lowndes County, and the black panther appeared on election ballots in contrast to the rooster of the Alabama Democratic Party, controlled by white supremacists. Later that fall, Carmichael announced plans to extend the LFCO model of an independent political party to other rural areas in the South, as well as to establish the party as a local organization that met the daily needs of poor and Black people. See John Hulett, "The Lowndes County Freedom Party," in *Black Protest: History, Documents, and Analyses,* ed. Joanne Grant (1968; rpt. New York: Fawcett/Ballantine, 1983). See also Kelley, *Hammer and Hoe,* and *The Eyes on the Prize Civil Rights Reader: Documents, Speeches, and Firsthand Accounts from the Black Freedom Struggle,* ed. Clayborne Carson et al. (New York: Penguin, 1991).

"Arise, ye slaves no more in thrall": Lines from the "Internationale," which became the anthem of communist parties throughout the world after it was written in the 1880s by Eugene Pottier and Pierre Degeyter to commemorate the 1871 Paris Commune. See Karl Marx, *The Civil War in France: The Paris Commune*, introduction by Frederick Engels (1891; rpt. New York: International Publishers, 1993).

"THE PETRIFIED WOMAN"

Epigraph from Angelo Herndon, "You Cannot Kill the Working Class," in *Black Protest*, ed. Joanne Grant, pp. 226, 232–33. Herndon, born in Cincinnati, Ohio, was arrested in Atlanta in 1932, at the age of nineteen, for organizing mass demonstrations to protest the suspension of public relief. The plaintiff in *Herndon v. Lowry*, 301 U.S. 242, the U.S. Supreme Court decision that overturned Georgia's insurrection statute, Herndon was freed after five years of national protest.

"Dora, Yolande, Belle Ellen": Mines in Bibb, Jefferson, Tuscaloosa, and Walker counties in Alabama, at the southern end of the Appalachian mountain range. The mineral deposits along the length of this range gave rise to coal mining, iron smelting, and steel mills from southwestern New York and western Pennsylvania through West Virginia, Kentucky, Tennessee, and Alabama.

"Copper Quechua men": Quechua miners, of Incan lineage, still work the Cerro Rico ("rich hill") in Potosí, in the Bolivian highlands. In the 1540s the Spanish colonial government forced indigenous peoples in Peru and Bolivia to slave in the mines. In the early decades of the system, four out of five miners died in their first year in the mines. The silver they produced had a profound impact on the world economy and enabled European elites to expand into an international market system. See Jack McIver Weatherford, *Indian Givers: How the Indians of the Americas Transformed the World* (New York: Fawcett Columbine, 1988).

"Black Sesotho men ... Irish men ... Colorado men": In South Africa, miners still work in gold mines opened in the late nineteenth century. Irishmen fleeing mid-nineteenth-century famine and British occupation were a significant portion of the laborers in the Pennsylvania coal fields. Since the 1880s, workers have dug lead, zinc, copper, silver, and gold out of the earth around Leadville, Colorado.

"Mauch Chunk": Some historians estimate that after the U.S. economic crash of 1873 only one-fifth of the work force was working regularly. The attempt to radically restructure the economy and improve the position of freed slaves in the Reconstruction South had been crushed. Troops that had occupied the South were withdrawn and used against striking workers in the North. After an 1875 strike in the coal mines of Schuylkill County, Pennsylvania, the most militant members of the Workingmen's Benevolent Association were arrested and sentenced to death on trumped-up charges. Nineteen men were hung. See Richard O. Boyer and Herbert M. Morais, *Labor's Untold Story* (New York: United Electrical, Radio and Machine Workers of America, 1955).

"One day our silence": The last words spoken by August Spies before he was hung in Chicago in 1887, along with three others convicted of conspiracy in a bombing at a rally of trade unionists, as quoted in Boyer and Morais, *Labor's Untold Story,* pp. 91–103. Union organizers had called this rally, held in Haymarket Square, to protest police violence against demonstrators on the day before; that May 1 rally was held by workers threatening a massive strike against local industrialists. Targeted and hung along with Spies as a leader in the fight for an eight-hour working day was Albert Parsons, a former Confederate soldier who had become a Radical Republican and was forced to flee the South during the terrors of the 1870s. He was the husband of Lucy Parsons (1853–1942), a socialist of African-American, Mexican, and Creek heritage active in union organizing. See Angela Davis, *Women, Race, and Class* (New York: Vintage/ Random House, 1983).

"Huakajchi": The mountain that has risen up beside the mine of Cerro Rico in Potosí, Bolivia. Huakajchi is built up out of the millions of tons of crushed rock that remains after the extraction of precious ores. See Weatherford, *Indian Givers.*

"THE SHRINE"

"Mary ... Kuan Yin": In Christianity, Mary is the Virgin Mother of God. In Buddhism, Kuan Yin is the human personification of compassion.

"Hum, Ma-Ma": A prayer to a Buddhist Mother of Wisdom, Sitatapatre. A *mudra,* a hand gesture in prayer, can indicate many different spiritual intentions and goals.

"FIGHTING FIRE"

"*Fuego ... Tenemos nada*": Fire ... We have nothing.

"THE FERRY"

Epigraph: Mae Lawrence was chairperson of a Mississippi Freedom Labor Union local involved in the 1966 occupation of a barracks at an air force base in Greenville. The MFLU was organized when sharecroppers striking for higher wages were evicted from their Delta plantations and were living in a tent city. Quoted in *Black Protest*, ed. Joanne Grant, p. 505.

"Farewell, Cahawba, Oka Aba ... Haysoppy": The Cahaba River of central Alabama was probably named *Oka Aba* ("water above") by people of the Choctaw Nation living on the lower course of the Alabama River. Haysoppy Creek, which flows into the Cahaba, may derive its name from the Choctaw *ush apa*, a term for a black gum tree with berries that birds love. See Rhoda Ellison, *Place Names of Bibb County, Alabama* (Brierfield, Ala.: Cahaba Trace Commission, 1993).

"If the dead could have counted": The words of Chief Cobb of the Choctaw Nation in Oklahoma in 1843, speaking of the forced removal of his people from the lands that became the states of Alabama and Mississippi. He is quoted in Angie Debo, *The Rise and Fall of the Choctaw Republic* (1934; rpt. Norman, Okla.: University of Oklahoma Press, 1961), p. 70. Centuries of European colonial warfare against Native-American nations culminated in the U.S. Indian Removal Act of 1830, which opened the frontier of the Southern territories to white cotton growers and other financial interests. White soldiers were offered land bounties for fighting in the "Creek Wars" of the removals. Despite resistance, the Cherokee, Chickasaw, Choctaw, and Creek Nations of the Southeast were driven from their lands by military force and economic coercion, into the territory that later became the state of Oklahoma. Nearly half the Creek Nation died during the journey or in their first few years in the West. A quarter of the Cherokee Nation died along what has come to be called "The Trail of Tears." See *Native American Testimony: A Chronicle of Indian-White Relations from Prophecy to the Present*, ed. Peter Nabokov (New York: Penguin, 1992).

"THE GREAT MIGRATION"

Epigraph from W. E. B. Du Bois, *Black Reconstruction in America: 1860–1880* (1935; rpt. New York: Atheneum, 1971), p. 706. William Edward Burghardt Du Bois (1868–1963) was the preeminent African-American intellectual of his century. What Du Bois termed "the counter revolution of property" by Northern industrialists and the old Southern slavocracy ended the radical Reconstruction of 1865–1877 in the South. The resulting oppressive conditions led to a mass migration of African Americans to Northern cities between 1900 and 1930. Later U. S. involvement in repression and economic exploitation has led to other migrations. In Chile, thousands fled into exile after a 1973 U.S.-sponsored coup ended in the death of Dr. Salvador Allende Gossens, democratically elected on a platform of full nationalization of all basic industries, banks, and communications. In the early 1980s, thousands of Guatemalans fled their homeland as the United States provided military aid to the government of General Rios Mott in its massacres of the civilian, mostly indigenous, population that supported a guerilla army fighting for land reform. In addition to Du Bois, see Jacqueline Jones, *Labor of Love, Labor of Sorrow: Black Women, Work, and the Family from Slavery to the Present* (New York: Vintage/Random House, 1986) and Sara Diamond, *Roads to Dominion: Right-Wing Movements and Political Power in the United States* (New York: The Guildford Press, 1995).

"De dónde eres tú?": Where are you from? "Las flores rojas, el puente": The red flowers, the bridge. "Crema de leche": Candy. "Del sur": From the South.

"The Great Migration": In 1941, African-American artist Jacob Lawrence (1917–) painted an epic series on this theme, "The Migration of the Negro." See Jacob Lawrence, *The Migration Series* (Washington, D.C.: Rappahannock, 1993).

"THE REMNANT SHOP"

Epigraph from Altagracia Ortiz, 'En la aguja y el pedal eché la hiel': Puerto Rican Women in the Garment Industry of New York City, 1920–1980," in *Puerto Rican Women and Work: Bridges in Transnational Labor,* ed. Altagracia Ortiz (Philadelphia: Temple University Press, 1996), pp. 55–81. Beginning in the 1950s, garment factories were relocated from New York City—first to New Jersey, Pennsylvania, Massachusetts, later to the southern United States and to Puerto Rico, Mexico, Haiti, the Dominican Republic, and the Philippines.

"From Ulaanbataar to Samarqand, through Lyon": Ulaanbataar, in Mongolia, and Samarqand, in Uzbekistan, are cities in Central Asia that were once stops on the Silk Road, a group of ancient trade routes by which raw silk was brought from China to the Mediterranean from the early 1200s until the mid 1980s. One end point of the trade was Lyon, France, where silk fabric production boomed with the invention of the Jacquard loom in 1804. Another end point was in the silk mills of Paterson, New Jersey, and nearby Hudson and Bergen Counties, in the early 1900s. This was the location of William Carlos Williams's epic poem *Paterson* (1958; rpt. New York: New Directions, 1963).

"The silk houses trembled": *Ikat* is a traditional pattern in silk weaving in Central Asia.

"In the Czar's plantations": In the early 1900s, in the Central Asian provinces of imperial Russia, czarist policy mandated the colonization of traditional nomadic grazing lands, and the replacement of traditional crops with cotton farmed through irrigation. On the eve of the 1917 Russian Revolution, peasants and nomadic tribes in Central Asia rebelled in a widespread revolt. See Richard Pipes, *The Formation of the Soviet Union: Communism and Nationalism, 1917–1923* (1954; rpt. Cambridge, Mass.: Harvard University Press, 1994), and Leon Trotsky, "The Proletariat and the Peasantry," in *The History of the Russian Revolution,* trans. Max Eastman (1932; rpt. New York: Monad Press, 1980).

"On Croix-Rousse hill": The *Canuts* (silk workers) of Lyon who lived and worked in this district rebelled in 1831 and 1834 against oppressive conditions brought on by increasing industrialization. Their motto was "To live by working, to die by fighting." The revolts were not completely put down until 1870. See *"De l'Empire a nos jours,"* at Centrale Lyon <www.ec-lyon.fr/tourism/Lyon/Histoire-Tradition/61.html.fr> and enter "Croix-Rousse" to take a virtual tour of the workers' district.

"Where in 1913 the company sheriff": In 1828, cotton weavers led the first strikes in the Paterson textile mills. By 1913, manufacturing there had turned to silk production, and the workers were Belgian, Dutch, English, French, German, Hungarian, Irish, Italian, Jewish, and Scot immigrants. In the 1913 Paterson strike, the most militant were the dyers, whose jobs were the most dangerous. See Eric Foner, *History of the Labor Movement in the United States,* vol. IV: *The Industrial Workers of the World 1905–1917* (New York: International Publishers, 1965), chap. 15, "The Paterson Strike," and *Rebel Voices: An I.W.W. Anthology,* ed. Joyce L. Kornbluh (Ann Arbor, Mich.: University of Michigan Press, 1964), chap. 7, "Paterson 1913."

"Down near Nanih Waiya": Located in Noxubee County, Mississippi, this flat-topped mound and nearby cave is a sacred site that, according to Choctaw traditions, is both the location to which the Choctaw Nation migrated from a land in the West, and the place where they emerged from the earth at Creation, along with the Creeks, the Cherokees, and the Chickasaws. See Israel Folsom, in

Native American Writing in the Southeast, 1875–1935 (Jackson, Miss.: University Press of Mississippi, 1995) and *Dictionary of Native American Mythology,* ed. Sam D. Gill and Irene F. Sullivan (New York: Oxford University Press, 1992).

"THE OTHER SIDE"

"Which is Mawu, which Lisa?": Audre Lorde describes Mawulisa as the female-male principle in the Dahomean traditions of West Africa. This deity is also sometimes called "the first, inseparable twins of the Creator of the Universe." See Lorde's notes to *The Black Unicorn* (New York: W. W. Norton, 1978).

Many people have helped me as I made my way through this work. My heartfelt thanks to all of you, including those unnamed here, especially those who spoke to me after readings or wrote to me about the poems. I would also like to gratefully acknowledge:

The women at the Pagoda poetry gathering, where the first of these poems were read, and in particular Adrienne Rich, for her comments then and later.

The women of the Conditions editorial collective who first published some of these poems—Dorothy Allison, Jan Clausen, Cheryl Clarke, Jewelle Gomez, Carroll Oliver, Mirtha Quintanales, Rima Shore—and especially Elly Bulkin for discussing this book with me from start to finish over fifteen years.

The women of the Feminary editorial collective during the time that I was a member—Susan Ballinger, Eleanor Holland, Helen Langa, Raymina Y. Mays, Mab Segrest, Cris South, and Aida Wakil.

The lesbian communities of Washington, D.C., and Atlanta, Georgia, as well as Lammas and Charis bookstores for creating and sustaining a place for writers like me and books like this.

In recent years, poet friends Elizabeth Alexander, Judith Arcana, Marilyn Chin, Cornelius Eady, Joy Harjo, Joan Larkin, Richard McCann for their encouragement—and Bino A. Realuyo for his insightful editing.

My agent Charlotte Sheedy, and Neeti Madan, for their continued support.

Ed Ochester and everyone at the University of Pittsburgh Press, for their fine work on this book.

My dear friends Nanette Gartrell, Holly Hughes, Dee Mosbacher, and Deirdre Sinnott.

My sons Ransom Weaver and Ben Weaver, for their love and conversation.

And my beloved, Leslie Feinberg—"In you, my end and my beginning."

Some of the poems in this book have appeared in slightly different versions in the following publications: *The American Voice* ("The Road to Selma"); *Bombay Gin* ("The A & P"); *Conditions* ("A Cold Not the Opposite of Life," "Out of Season," "Red String," "Shades," "Walking Back Up Depot Street"); *Feminary* ("Bust of Martha Mitchell to Be Unveiled," "Painting Her Fingernails Red"); *Gargoyle* ("The Ferry"); *New England Review* ("At Deep Midnight"); *New*

England Review/Bread Loaf Quarterly ("Strange Flesh"); *North Carolina Literary Review* ("On the Silver Coast"); *Ploughshares* ("The White Star"); *Prairie Schooner* ("The Great Migration," "Second Sight," "Snake Eyes," "Swingblade," "What the Cat Knows"); *River Styx* ("Eating Clay").

"The Other Side" first appeared in *TriQuarterly,* a publication of Northwestern University.

Minnie Bruce Pratt, a white anti-racist author and activist, was raised in the segregated South. She co-authored *Yours in Struggle: Three Feminist Perspectives on Anti-Semitism and Racism* with Elly Bulkin and Barbara Smith. Pratt's second book of poetry, *Crime Against Nature,* was chosen as the 1989 Lamont Poetry Selection by the Academy of American Poets, was nominated for a Pulitzer Prize, and received the American Library Association's Gay and Lesbian Book Award for Literature. Her other books include *The Sound of One Fork, We Say We Love Each Other, Rebellion: Essays 1980–1991,* and *S/HE,* stories about gender boundary crossing. Her web address is <www.mbpratt.org>.